daily
bread
teeN bible studies

PARABLES
OF JESUS

FLORIDA COLLEGE
PRESS

Parables of Jesus
Daily Bread Teen Bible Studies
Copyright © 2025
Florida College Press
119 N. Glen Arven Ave.
Temple Terrace, Florida 33617

ISBN: 978-1-965356-01-2

Printed in the United States of America.

Images for the cover and the lessons from various artists at pexels.com

INTRODUCTION TO THE
DAILY BREAD SERIES

There are few things more foundational for life than "daily bread." All of us wake up hungry, spend the day hunting down food, enjoy a well-prepared supper, and finish our days snacking in fear that we'll get hungry at night. Many of us live to eat instead of eat to live, and it shows when we step on those bathroom scales. For most of us, our hunger is based less on need and more on habit.

What if we felt the same love and desperation for spiritual food? What if we woke up hungry to hear from God, spent the day searching out His truth, and longed for that well-prepared feast of ideas in the evening, and even wanted a few snacks before going to bed? While that might sound exaggerated, it certainly is worth considering.

In this series of books, we want to help you create some good habits that will leave you longing for more of God's Word. We encourage a deeper desire to find new truths and wrestle with more ideas from God's Word. Join us as we learn to not only open God's Word, but to do so regularly and with excitement. We want to create a dependency of finding God's answers for today's questions.

Each lesson is designed to be used personally. While each book will have some helpful instructions for using them in a class setting, our deeper desire is to give young people the resources to create habits that will serve them for life and to find themselves eager to learn more about the New Testament. We want these books in the hands of every young seeker so that they can be better prepared to face life with God's answers.

This book is a special study in the Daily Bread series, which does not have a daily requirement for being in God's Word, but is a special study on small sections of scripture. These lessons can be completed in one sitting, but our encouragement is to allow these lessons to challenge your thought for several days. Use these lessons for reflection and growth.

A COMPLETE
LIST OF **PARABLES** FROM THE
SYNOPTIC GOSPELS

		Matthew	Mark	Luke	#
1	Counting the Cost			14.28-33	14
2	Dragnet	13.47-50			18
3	Fig Tree	24.32-35	13.28-29	21.29-31	22
4	Friend Seeking Bread			11.5-8	26
5	Good Samaritan			10.30-37	30
6	Great Banquet			14.16-24	34
7	Growing Seed		4.26-29		38
8	Treasure and Pearl	13.44-46			42
9	Homeowner	13.52			46
10	Lamp Stand	5.14-16	4.21-22	8.16	50
11	Leaven	13.33		13.20-21	54
12	Lost (Prodigal) Son			15.11-32	58
14	Lost Coin			15.8-10	64
14	Lost Sheep	18.10-14		15.3-7	68
15	Master & Servant			17.7-10	72
16	Moneylender			7.41-43	76
17	Mustard Seed	13.31-32	4.30-32	13.18-19	80
18	Narrow Door			13.23-30	84
19	The New Cloth & Wineskin	9:16-17	2.21-22	5.36-38	88
20	Persistent Widow			18.2-8	92

INTRODUCTION TO THE
PARABLES

The parables are fascinating studies, full of surprises and details that are easy to miss when read quickly in a study of the gospels. Each story has specific details unique to when Jesus tells it as He crafted stories to aid in His teaching. We tend to consider the parable the easy part of Jesus's sermons, almost as if they are illustrations intended to give examples and help the listener understand His message more clearly. This is an incorrect way to understand these rich and complicated stories.

Jesus explains to His disciples that He did not tell these stories to make things easier. When asked why He spoke in parables, Jesus answers:

> "Because the secrets of the kingdom of heaven have been given for you to know, but it has not been given to them. For whoever has, more will be given to him, and he will have more than enough; but whoever does not have, even what he has will be taken away from him. That is why I speak to them in parables, because looking they do not see, and hearing they do not listen or understand (Matt 13.11-13).

Jesus was not making things easier by telling quips and stories. Instead, He kept the hidden things hidden from those who were unprepared to hear them. He guarded the message from those unwilling to hear it.

This becomes important in Jesus's ministry. He was going to make a lot of enemies before it was all said and done. He became known as the rabbi who publicly rebuked the religious elite. He would tell the Sadducees that they were ignorant of the Scriptures. He would call Pharisees hypocrites and a brood of vipers. He would call out the Sanhedrin as disobedient and unrighteous. His stories would eventually get the religious leaders angry because Jesus would call attention to the history of their ancestors who abused and persecuted the prophets of old. Through His parables, he would even claim to be the Son of God. For those who did not want to accept Jesus as Christ, the parables were often Jesus's way of keeping them in the dark. He was not going to force anyone to accept Him as the promised Anointed One if they did not want to receive God's gift to mankind.

POSITIVE REASONS FOR PARABLES

That being said, Jesus's stories would certainly have been helpful for those looking for answers and wanting to know more about the Kingdom of God. Stories, as a general rule, are easy to remember. When these people went home after hearing one of Jesus's stories, they could easily relay those stories to others and discuss the finer points of Jesus's teachings. These parables would have made difficult teachings more accessible for those seeking answers.

Jesus would have been teaching many who were uneducated who would relate well to the stories. They knew shepherds. They grew crops. They picked figs from trees and understood the role of servants. When Jesus spoke about the common man, it would have encouraged the ordinary worker or the slave. They would feel seen and loved. They would feel appreciated, especially as Jesus often used His parables to call out the elite and exalted. Jesus exalted the humble and humbled the exalted.

These parables also made Jesus's teachings more accessible to the illiterate. Jesus did not write tomes where he parced languages and dissected passages. Instead, He told stories. In an aural and oral culture, this was especially important. They learned by hearing and discussing, and Jesus's stories would have given them much to chew on as they discussed His teachings. He told stories that allowed them to consume an entire message and be able to share it with others.

Lastly, Jesus's parables would have been cryptic. As stated before, this was intentional for those who did not honestly want to understand, but in some ways, it would be true even for those who did. How many times did the disciples ask Jesus to explain what He meant in a story or why He told parables instead of being plain? At one point, the disciples even exclaimed, "Look, now you're speaking plainly and not using any figurative language. Now we know that you know everything and don't need anyone to question you. By this we believe that you came from God" (John 16.29-30). Jesus replied, "Sorry guys. You still don't get it" (*author's paraphrase*). Jesus's stories would have been confusing, but that is good in that it would have given them much to discuss and dwell on as disciples. They could toss ideas back and forth as they grew and developed into disciples who would take His teachings to the world.

PARABLES TODAY

Today, we are left to decide whether or not we want to understand God's Word. We can keep our hands over our eyes and ears, refusing to hear God's Word. We can fail to understand these parables like those Jewish leaders of Jesus's day.

Or we can be diligent disciples willing to dig deeply into these great stories created by Jesus and search them for Jesus's truths. We are left with the choice.

DIGGING INTO THE PARABLES

Context matters when it comes to the parables. Each lesson will begin with the same context questions. Answer these before you read the parable (or as you read the parables). You will need your Bibles to accomplish this task.

Second, dig into the text. Guiding questions are provided to help you observe the details of the parables. These questions are by no means comprehensive, but they will point you to important details.

Third, read the additional thoughts. These are sometimes about the entire parable and sometimes about a detail, but they are designed to help you think about an aspect that you might or might not have noticed.

Fourth, think through the thought questions. Don't give the most straightforward answer. Instead, think through all the answers you can think of. Make sure you get as much out of the parables as possible.

Lastly, feel free to discuss these parables with others. Stories have a way of coming alive through discussion and telling the parable again and again. Use your friends and mentors to help you learn as much as possible. These stories are given for our growth, but how much you grow with them is dependent on how much work you are willing to put into them. Let these stories become part of the daily bread on which you feed and grow your soul.

PARABLES

EARTHLY STORIES WITH HEAVENLY MEANINGS

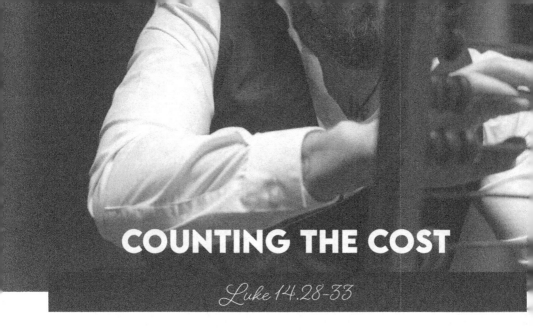

COUNTING THE COST

Luke 14.28-33

Is there any context for this story? If so, what is it?

Who is speaking and to whom?

Are there other parables around this one or is this one on its own?

Identify where in Jesus's ministry you would place this parable and explain why.
  Beginning • Galilean Ministry • Judean Ministry • Final Weeks

Read the parable in two different translations and note any differences below.

Stories evoke feelings. What overall feeling does this story give you?

28 "For which of you, wanting to build a tower, doesn't first sit down and calculate the cost to see if he has enough to complete it? 29 Otherwise, after he has laid the foundation and cannot finish it, all the onlookers will begin to ridicule him, 30 saying, 'This man started to build and wasn't able to finish.'

Why would this man be ridiculed?

Which is harder – making a plan or adjusting to failures? Why?

31 "Or what king, going to war against another king, will not first sit down and decide if he is able with ten thousand to oppose the one who comes against him with twenty thousand? 32 If not, while the other is still far off, he sends a delegation and asks for terms of peace. 33 In the same way, therefore, every one of you who does not renounce all his possessions cannot be my disciple.

Who should win this battle between the kings?

What is a delegation?

Why would this king ask for peace if he wants to go to war?

What is the point of this parable in your own words?

The parables of Jesus were filled with incredible and easily imagined characters and conundrums. This parable's embarrassing situations are relatable. Many of us have reached the end of a project and found ourselves short of materials or misjudged our strength when lifting weights. Before we began the project or the workout, we should have judged with wisdom and avoided regret for our misfortune.

This is doubly true when it comes to following Jesus. Before we consider discipleship, we must count the cost. We must consider how much we are willing to give to belong to Him. We must be willing to sacrifice if we are going to belong to the Sacrifice.

Those who do not might find themselves in a worse state than had they never known the Lord in the first place (cf. 2 Pet 2.20-22). Peter left this "worse state" undefined, but considering this was the apostle who saw the crucified Lord, we can understand he knew a little about counting the cost. This is the same Peter who is told that he will die for his discipleship (cf. Joh 21.18-19). This is the same Peter who spends much time talking about sacrifices and persecution in his letter (cf. 1 Pet 3.17-22; 4.12-19).

Jesus clearly states that following Him carries some costs. He specifically mentions giving up possessions. What will you give up for Him?

ADDITIONAL THOUGHTS

What possible sacrifices exist when choosing to follow Jesus? What costs are a part of being His disciple?

Why will it be worse for those who knew the Lord to turn their backs on following Him (cf. 2 Pet 2.20-22)?

What do we gain by being a disciple of Jesus? Is what we gain worth what we might have to sacrifice?

THOUGHT QUESTIONS

Whoever does not bear his own cross and come after me cannot be my disciple.

Luke 14.27

DRAGNET

Matthew 13:47-50

Is there any context for this story? If so, what is it?

Who is speaking and to whom?

Are there other parables around this one or is this one on its own?

Identify where in Jesus's ministry you would place this parable and explain why.

Beginning • Galilean Ministry • Judean Ministry • Final Weeks

Read the parable in two different translations and note any differences below.

47 "Again, the kingdom of heaven is like a large net thrown into the sea. It collected every kind of fish, 48 and when it was full, they dragged it ashore, sat down, and gathered the good fish into containers, but threw out the worthless ones. 49 So it will be at the end of the age. The angels will go out, separate the evil people from the righteous, 50 and throw them into the blazing furnace, where there will be weeping and gnashing of teeth.

What overall feeling does this story give you?

What is a dragnet?

Can you think of a time when a net became full in Scripture? Give the reference.

What does the net catch?

What happens to the fish?

How will this happen? What details do we learn about God's plans?

When will this happen?

There is sometimes confusion about what the "kingdom of heaven" is talking about, but the clues reveal the answer. As Jesus went about preaching, He often taught "the Gospel of the Kingdom" (cf. Mat 4.23), which is then delivered to us in the form of the Sermon on the Mount (Mat 5-7). Many of the stories He tells in the gospel of Matthew are about this same kingdom.

This story reveals that this kingdom does not merely exist once we enter our inheritance (i.e., heaven) but is something that we enter into before the end. It is a place where there are good and evil (fish, sheep vs. goats, etc.). Simply put, the "kingdom of heaven" is where the King reigns. This is the Church.

As you encounter parables about the kingdom of heaven, force yourself to think correctly and identify these parables about the church. In the church, God has thrown out the net. He is bringing all types into His Church: Jews, Gentiles, males and females, and people from all walks of life. Backgrounds, races, cultures, or histories do not matter. God brings them all in.

In the end, when the "harvest" or "gathering" or "judgment" is here, God will sort through the "kingdom of heaven" and bring into heaven those He judges as truly belonging to Him. May we be in that number.

What is required to be in the number of "good fish" or saved by God? What standard does God use for sorting the fish?

Was the point of this parable to emphasize the "good and bad" would be gathered together, or that we think some are good and some are bad but have to trust God to sort it out? Explain your answer.

What you do know about the place where "there will be weeping and gnashing of teeth?" Explain and give references to other passages.

"Follow me," he told them, "and I will
make you fish for people."
Matthew 4.19

FIG TREE

Matthew 24:32-35; Mark 13:28-29; Luke 21:29-31

Is there any context for this story? If so, what is it?

Who is speaking and to whom?

Are there other parables around this one or is this one on its own?

Identify where in Jesus's ministry you would place this parable and explain why.
   Beginning • Galilean Ministry • Judean Ministry • Final Weeks

Read the parable in two different translations and note any differences below.

TEXT

32 "Learn this lesson from the fig tree: As soon as its branch becomes tender and sprouts leaves, you know that summer is near. 33 In the same way, when you see all these things, recognize that he is near—at the door. 34 Truly I tell you, this generation will certainly not pass away until all these things take place. 35 Heaven and earth will pass away, but my words will never pass away.

QUESTIONS

What overall feeling does this story give you?

Name some distinguishing characteristics of a fig tree.

What does the fig tree help someone know?

What else can we watch to know that "he is near?"

When he gets near, where does he wait?

Using the context, who is "he?"

When will these things happen?

Sometimes, parables stand alone as complete teachings. Other times, the parables read more like sermon illustrations, dependent on the context of the sermon around it. The fig tree parable is more of a sermon illustration, emphasizing to the listeners that the Son of Man was coming soon and that redemption was coming soon. There is much debate as to whether Jesus is speaking of the end of times and the destruction of the earth or if he is teaching more specifically about the destruction of Jerusalem itself. In either case, the parable serves the same purpose, as if He is saying, "If you pay attention, you'll see it coming."

In other places, the Bible writers will tell us to be "sober-minded" and "watchful" (cf. Mat 26.41; 1 The 5.6; Tit 2.2, 6, 12; 1 Pet 1.13; 4.7; 5.8) to prepare for temptation, godly action, end of all things, and the prowling devil. Jesus continues in Matthew to tell the Parable of the Ten Virgins. Jesus is concerned that we know what is happening so we can best be prepared for our challenges as His disciples.

The fig tree would serve as a reminder to these early disciples, whenever they saw one, that they were to be mindful of what God was doing in the world around them. They were to be watchful and alert. They were to focus on God's things instead of their own.

While Jesus used a fig tree to prove his point, what other reminders do we have around us that can serve the same purpose? Rewrite this parable for modern times.

If the event Jesus is speaking about happened while those who were living then were still alive, does this parable have any message for us today? Explain your answer.

If we cannot know when Jesus is coming, why should we be watchful for it? How should we "recognize that he is near?"

"This is why you are also to be ready, because the Son of Man is coming at an hour you do not expect."

Matthew 24.44

FRIEND SEEKING BREAD

Luke 11:5-8

Is there any context for this story? If so, what is it?

Who is speaking and to whom?

Are there other parables around this one or is this one on its own?

Identify where in Jesus's ministry you would place this parable and explain why.

Beginning • Galilean Ministry • Judean Ministry • Final Weeks

Read the parable in two different translations and note any differences below.

5 He also said to them, "Suppose one of you has a friend and goes to him at midnight and says to him, 'Friend, lend me three loaves of bread, 6 because a friend of mine on a journey has come to me, and I don't have anything to offer him.' 7 Then he will answer from inside and say, 'Don't bother me! The door is already locked, and my children and I have gone to bed. I can't get up to give you anything.' 8 I tell you, even though he won't get up and give him anything because he is his friend, yet because of his friend's shameless boldness, he will get up and give him as much as he needs.

TEXT

QUESTIONS

What overall feeling does this story give you?

Explain this parable in your own words.

When the friend asked for bread, what response does he get?

Why does the friend need more bread?

Which friend do you think was in the right and who was in the wrong?

Why does the friend eventually get out of bed and share his bread?

What is the point of this parable?

First-century Israel was a culture of hospitality, and bread was a staple of life in every home. It was always available. There was nothing fancy about it. It was a basic offering. The idea that a house would have no bread when out-of-town visitors came calling was probably a common situation to which all of the people could relate. Borrowing bread from a neighbor or friend would also have been expected in a culture of hospitality.

What is unexpected is for someone to refuse to share. He certainly had valid reasons. It was the middle of the night. He was asleep, and this man was disturbing his family. But the man's bold determination to get some bread eventually forced him out of bed to grab some bread, open the door, and thrust it into his arms. A little crankiness goes a long way.

This parable is somewhat unexpected in our modern-day etiquette. We would not dream of disturbing someone's sleep and rudely persisting after we've been told no. Seemingly, Jesus is saying this is the right thing to do. Yet, the point is not to be rude, but as we can see from the context, we are to be persistent in prayer. We should continually go to God, ask for what we need, and continue to ask because we know we are praying to a God who gives.

What lessons can we learn from this parable other than persistence in prayer?

When we have a need, what is the first thing we do? Where do we first go for help? How can we put God as the focus on those moments?

How can we show "shameless boldness" to God while making sure we are not crossing the line into disrespect or selfishness?

""I am the bread of life," Jesus told them. "No one who comes to me will ever be hungry, and no one who believes in me will ever be thirsty again."

John 6.35

GOOD SAMARITAN

Luke 10.30-35

Is there any context for this story? If so, what is it?

Who is speaking and to whom?

Are there other parables around this one or is this one on its own?

Identify where in Jesus's ministry you would place this parable and explain why.

   Beginning • Galilean Ministry • Judean Ministry • Final Weeks

Read the parable in two different translations and note any differences below.

30 Jesus took up the question and said, "A man was going down from Jerusalem to Jericho and fell into the hands of robbers. They stripped him, beat him up, and fled, leaving him half dead. 31 A priest happened to be going down that road. When he saw him, he passed by on the other side. 32 In the same way, a Levite, when he arrived at the place and saw him, passed by on the other side. 33 But a Samaritan on his journey came up to him, and when he saw the man, he had compassion. 34 He went over to him and bandaged his wounds, pouring on olive oil and wine. Then he put him on his own animal, brought him to an inn, and took care of him. 35 The next day he took out two denarii, gave them to the innkeeper, and said, 'Take care of him. When I come back I'll reimburse you for whatever extra you spend.'

What overall feeling does this story give you?

What is a Samaritan?

What did the priest do?

What did the Levite do?

What did the Samaritan do?

If you were a Jew listening to Jesus tell this story, what would be your reaction to the actions of the Samaritan?

Explain how generous the Samaritan acted?

Jesus often made heroes out of the unlovable, so he used the Samaritans in his parables, not because they were terrible people but because the Jews listening to his stories despised their northern neighbors.

The contrast between the Samaritan and the others is the most astonishing part of this parable. The Samaritan did what you would expect a Levite and priest to do. Certainly, they justified their inaction. They were ceremonially cleaned. They had a job to do. They were busy.

Yet, Jesus specifically tells us that the Samaritan was on a journey. He had somewhere to be. He was not just walking outside the city. He had a long distance to travel. Yet, he cleared room on his donkey, picked up a beaten and bloodied man, and transported him to where someone could nurse him back to health. He paid for his healing and provided for his needs.

It is hard not to think of another similar situation that would happen soon after Jesus tells this story. Jesus would be the despised one. Jesus would be beaten and bloodied. The Levites and priests would overlook Jesus. When we relate this to Jesus, he is both the beaten man and the caretaker, He did it all for us. He pays the price for our healing and ensures we are nursed back to spiritual health.

Why was Jesus asked, "Who is my neighbor?"

Did Jesus answer the question he was asked? Do you think they understood the point?

Can you name "good Samaritans" throughout the Bible? Give five examples and explain why they were "good Samaritans."

"'Then Jesus told him, "Go and do the same."

Luke 10.37b

GREAT BANQUET

Luke 14:16-24

Is there any context for this story? If so, what is it?

Who is speaking and to whom?

Are there other parables around this one or is this one on its own?

Identify where in Jesus's ministry you would place this parable and explain why.

  Beginning • Galilean Ministry • Judean Ministry • Final Weeks

Read the parable in two different translations and note any differences below.

16 Then he told him, "A man was giving a large banquet and invited many. 17 At the time of the banquet, he sent his servant to tell those who were invited, 'Come, because everything is now ready.'

18 "But without exception they all began to make excuses. The first one said to him, 'I have bought a field, and I must go out and see it. I ask you to excuse me.'

19 "Another said, 'I have bought five yoke of oxen, and I'm going to try them out. I ask you to excuse me.'

20 "And another said, 'I just got married, and therefore I'm unable to come.'

21 "So the servant came back and reported these things to his master. Then in anger, the master of the house told his servant, 'Go out quickly into the streets and alleys of the city, and bring in here the poor, maimed, blind, and lame.'

22 "'Master,' the servant said, 'what you ordered

What overall feeling does this story give you?

What does the master tell his servant to do?

What is the first excuse?

What is the second excuse?

What is the third excuse?

What does the master do since none of the invited will come?

What is peculiar about those who were invited the second time?

What is the problem once they have brought in many guests?

Where is the servant supposed to go to find guests?

What is the master's goal?

What does the master say about those who were originally invited to his banquet?

has been done, and there's still room.'

23 "Then the master told the servant, 'Go out into the highways and hedges and make them come in, so that my house may be filled. 24 For I tell you, not one of those people who were invited will enjoy my banquet.'"

The guests make excuses as to why they cannot come.

The first has bought a field and must see it. This seems odd because who among us would make such a major purchase without having seen what we were buying? It is possible that this is the point. This man represents the wealthy, the local business owner, the man of means and reputation. He makes purchases not because they are wise but because he can. He cares more about himself than his friend.

The second has purchased oxen and must try them. Again, this seems odd because who among us would purchase work equipment without knowing what we were buying? Who among us would go to work in a field instead of sitting at a table laden with food with a friend? This man is distracted and driven. He cares much about success, but he cares little about relationships.

The third has married. This seems like a great reason to miss hanging out with a friend, but how is the master, his friend, just now hearing about this? All his friends would have been invited to his wedding if he had married. This man has no relationship with the master.

None of these have a relationship with the master that they value. Therefore, it is easy for them to make excuses.

Do we have a relationship with the Master, or do we also make excuses?

What excuses will we make that will justify not coming to the Master when he calls us?

Why did the master invite in stangers? What point is this parable making? Consider what you know about Jews and Gentiles.

Why is it important that the master's table be filled? Consider the contrast presented in verses 23 and 24.

GROWING SEED

Mark 4.26-29

Is there any context for this story? If so, what is it?

Who is speaking and to whom?

Are there other parables around this one or is this one on its own?

Identify where in Jesus's ministry you would place this parable and explain why.

Beginning • Galilean Ministry • Judean Ministry • Final Weeks

Read the parable in two different translations and note any differences below.

26 "The kingdom of God is like this," he said. "A man scatters seed on the ground. 27 He sleeps and rises night and day; the seed sprouts and grows, although he doesn't know how. 28 The soil produces a crop by itself—first the blade, then the head, and then the full grain on the head. 29 As soon as the crop is ready, he sends for the sickle, because the harvest has come."

What overall feeling does this story give you?

What is the kingdom of God? Explain your answer.

What does the farmer do?

What does the farmer not know?

What process does the seed go through?

Once the crop is ready, what does the farmer do?

Who does know how the seed grows?

First-century Israel was an agricultural society full of farmers, shepherds, and vineyard workers. These occupations are mentioned often in Scripture, and many of the most well-known men and women in the Bible spent their days doing them. It makes sense that Jesus would use these agricultural ideas in many of his parables.

The growing process of a plant would have been familiar to almost everyone on that day, even if it is less understood today by the average man or woman. They had placed seeds in the ground and watched them grow. They knew that plants do not sprout overnight. They knew a field was broken up and plowed before seeds were planted. They knew they would produce healthier plants after days of care, watering, and fertilizing. They knew what seedlings looked like. They knew leaves would stripe, wilt, or curl whenever something was wrong with the growing process.

Yet, as much as they knew, they still did not know what God knew about the growing process, whether germination, pollination, or cultivation. They knew what they needed to know to bring the seed to harvest. That was enough.

Sometimes, knowing some and trusting God with the rest is all that is needed. That will get us to the harvest.

What is the point of this parable?

Why do we want to know more than we know? What does Deu 29.29 teach us about this?

What are some things you wish the Bible told us more about? How can you learn more about these things?

You have been born again—
not of perishable seed but of
imperishable—through the living
and enduring word of God. For,
All flesh is like grass,
and all its glory like a flower of
the grass.
The grass withers, and the flower
falls, but the word of the Lord
endures forever.
And this word is the gospel that
was proclaimed to you.

1 Peter 1.23-25

TREASURE AND PEARLS

Matthew 13:44-46

Is there any context for this story? If so, what is it?

Who is speaking and to whom?

Are there other parables around this one or is this one on its own?

Identify where in Jesus's ministry you would place this parable and explain why.

Beginning • Galilean Ministry • Judean Ministry • Final Weeks

Read the parable in two different translations and note any differences below.

⁴⁴ "The kingdom of heaven is like treasure, buried in a field, that a man found and reburied. Then in his joy he goes and sells everything he has and buys that field.

⁴⁵ "Again, the kingdom of heaven is like a merchant in search of fine pearls. ⁴⁶ When he found one priceless pearl, he went and sold everything he had and bought it.

What overall feeling does this story give you?

What is the "kingdom of heaven?"

What was found in both parables?

What did the man do in the first parable?

What does the man do in the second parable?

Name similarities between these two stories.

Name some differences between these two stories.

What is the point of these parables?

There is a chance to be distracted in both of these short parables. At first, it seems selfish that a man would find a treasure, bury it again, and buy the field, all so that he can have it to himself. This seems entirely self-serving. The second story says that the treasure is priceless, but it clearly has a price because when he sells everything he has, he has enough to purchase the pearl.

But these arguments miss the point. The point in both parables is that the treasure is worth everything. It is worth keeping safe until it is owned. It is worth everything you own to own it. The treasure should be valued above all else.

What is the treasure? It's identified in both parables. It is the "kingdom of heaven," where God reigns as king. It is the eternal kingdom. It is the community of God's people. It is the collection of saved souls throughout history and the future. It is the Church.

This is where truth is found, salvation is abundant, and hope is realized. It is the God-fearing, Bible-hearing, Heaven-nearing saints. While we cannot own that like a treasure in a hole or a pearl from the sea, it is certainly something we can participate in if we seek God's will and salvation. God, through His grace, desires that all be saved (1 Tim 2.3-4; Tit 2.11), and we can have that treasure if we will just go to Him.

Why would you say that God's Word, Way, and Will are treasures?

If God is King in this "kingdom of heaven," what are we? What does this mean?

What are you personally willing to give up to have God's treasure? What is worth more than this?

But seek first the kingdom of God and his righteousness, and all these things will be provided for you.

Matthew 6.33

HOMEOWNER

Matthew 13:52

Is there any context for this story? If so, what is it?

Who is speaking and to whom?

Are there other parables around this one or is this one on its own?

Identify where in Jesus's ministry you would place this parable and explain why.

Beginning • Galilean Ministry • Judean Ministry • Final Weeks

Read the parable in two different translations and note any differences below.

TEXT

51 "Have you understood all these things?"

They answered him, "Yes."

52 "Therefore," he said to them, "every teacher of the law who has become a disciple in the kingdom of heaven is like the owner of a house who brings out of his storeroom treasures new and old."

QUESTIONS

What overall feeling does this story give you?

Jesus talks about teachers of the law. What do we know about teachers of the law from the days of Jesus?

What new and old treasures would a house contain?

Why would an owner bring out these new and old treasures?

In talking about new and old treasures to teachers of the law, it is likely focusing on new and old teachings in the law. Read the next story in Matthew 13 and see how this is enacted. Write down what happens here.

Does this still apply today?

During Jesus's time, teachers of the Law focused on the old teachings. They wanted to know what the lawyers, rabbis, and experts of the past would say. They were often followers of teachers as they sought to understand the Law.

Jesus did not teach like this. Matthew even makes a point in saying, "When Jesus had finished saying these things, the crowds were astonished at his teaching, because he was teaching them like one who had authority, and not like their scribes" (7.28-29). In this sermon (Mat 5-7), Jesus revisited the Law and mentioned multiple times that they had misunderstood it and needed to understand better what God had initially intended. He would say, "You have heard," followed by," but I tell you," and then reveal some new understanding. Jesus cared deeply about the "old" treasures, but He was unafraid of "new" treasures as long as they came from God.

This does not mean we are waiting for a new revelation. God has revealed everything needed (2 Pet 1.3; Jud 3). Yet, even within the "old" treasures are fresh treasures unfound–maybe not to anyone before, but treasures we have not personally yet uncovered. We need to diligently seek God's truths. "The truth will set you free" (Joh 8.32). If we want to experience the freedom of the kingdom of heaven, start with the truth.

Are we still supposed to be finding new and old teachings in the law? Explain your answer.

What dangers exists when seeking "new" treasures? What dangers exist when seeking "old" treasures from God's Word?

How does one become a disciple in the kingdom of heaven? Use other passages to support your answer.

All Scripture is breathed out by God and profitable for teaching, for reproof, for correction, and for training in righteousness, that the man of God may be complete, equipped for every good work.

2 Tim 3.16-17

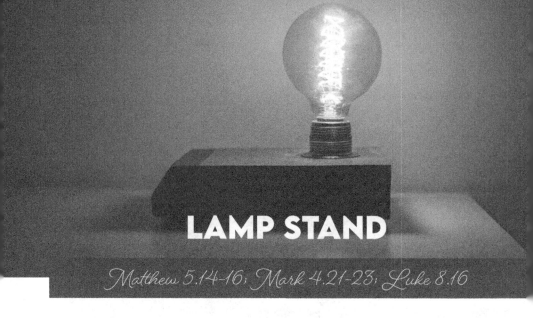

LAMP STAND

Matthew 5.14-16; Mark 4.21-23; Luke 8.16

Is there any context for this story? If so, what is it?

Who is speaking and to whom?

Are there other parables around this one or is this one on its own?

Identify where in Jesus's ministry you would place this parable and explain why.

Beginning • Galilean Ministry • Judean Ministry • Final Weeks

Read the parable in two different translations and note any differences below.

What overall feeling does this story give you?

Why do people light lamps?

How were their lights/lamps different than our modern lights?

²¹ He also said to them, "Is a lamp brought in to be put under a basket or under a bed? Isn't it to be put on a lampstand? ²² For there is nothing hidden that will not be revealed, and nothing concealed that will not be brought to light. ²³ If anyone has ears to hear, let him listen."

Why would someone put a light under a basket?

What dangers exist by putting a light under a bed?

What does verse 23 mean?

Name other passages in the Bible that use the idea of light to teach a lesson.

In a world without light pollution, nighttime was dark. Many of us today, especially in America, live where even the darkness of night is still pretty bright. We cannot see the stars they could see. We cannot experience darkness like they did. Darkness does not have the same level of fear today since we can flick a button and have light all around us or a flashlight shining far in front of us. Light was a commodity, and lamps were important.

Therefore, lamps make a great illustration. Everyone had some and used them often. The small open flame of an oil lamp was a welcome companion if you worked around the house at nighttime. These lamps were not lit and then put under a basket so they did not put out as much light. They put out a limited amount of light in the first place. Yet, having that small flame made everything visible.

Just like that, God's Word shines a light on the world around it. It reveals sins for those hearing its words when it talks about sin. When it talks about hope, it gives hope to those obeying its message. When it talks about God, it reveals God as we see Him active among the stories of Scripture. We depend on God's Word to reveal truth about spiritual things and the world itself. God's Word shines a light on the truth of everything it touches.

Compare the three tellings of this parable from each Gospel. Do they have different messages based on the context?

Is this parable intended to create positive or negative feelings? Explain your answer.

If everything we did was revealed to the world around us, would that change how we act? What about our thoughts; would that change anything?

Your word is a lamp to my feet
and a light to my path.

Psalm 119.105

LEAVEN

Matthew 13.33; Luke 13.20-21

Is there any context for this story? If so, what is it?

Who is speaking and to whom?

Are there other parables around this one or is this one on its own?

Identify where in Jesus's ministry you would place this parable and explain why.

Beginning • Galilean Ministry • Judean Ministry • Final Weeks

Read the parable in two different translations and note any differences below.

20 Again he said, "What can I compare the kingdom of God to? 21 It's like leaven that a woman took and mixed into fifty pounds of flour until all of it was leavened."

TEXT

QUESTIONS

What overall feeling does this story give you?

By way of reminder, what is the "kingdom of God?"

What is leaven?

What did the woman do with the leaven?

Why so much flour?

How much leaven is needed for 50 pounds of flour?

Was this an inordinate amout of dough making? What would make this amount of bread understandable?

Leaven is an interesting idea in the Scriptures. In some passages, it is a good thing, like this parable. In other places, teachers use it to illustrate bad things. God commanded the Jews to sweep out their houses and rid themselves of all leaven for the Feast of Passover and Feast of Unleavened Bread (Exo 12.15). Grain offerings could not be made with leaven (Lev 2.11). False teaching and sin in the church are described as leaven (Mat 16.6-12; 1 Cor 5.1-8). The common idea is that false teaching and sin tend to spread and affect the whole, as leaven does the dough, and therefore need to be dealt with immediately.

Leaven does not represent good or evil but illustrates something that spreads. In the case of this parable, the "kingdom of heaven" is supposed to spread. And it did. Jesus commanded that this happen (Mat 28.19-20; Acts 1.8). Then, consider the work of the apostles in the Book of Acts and statements like Acts 9.31 and 17.6. The kingdom of heaven multiplied and affected the entire world. This happened because the early Christians went about talking about Jesus and teaching those with whom they came into contact (Act 8.4). The truth and Word of God spread like leaven through the lump of dough. When God's people get excited about God's Word, it will spread everywhere.

Does the gospel look like leaven today? Is it spreading like leaven anymore? Explain your answer.

What would be necessary to get the kingdom of heaven spreading like that again?

nIf the woman is making a lot of bread with her leaven, what is she likely intending to do with the bread? Are there any lessons from this detail of the parable? Explain your answer.

A little leaven leavens the whole batch of dough...
Galatians 5.9

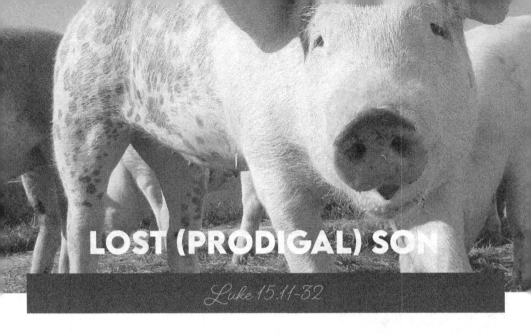

LOST (PRODIGAL) SON

Luke 15:11-32

Is there any context for this story? If so, what is it?

Who is speaking and to whom?

Are there other parables around this one or is this one on its own?

Identify where in Jesus's ministry you would place this parable and explain why.

Beginning • Galilean Ministry • Judean Ministry • Final Weeks

Read the parable in two different translations and note any differences below.

TEXT

[11] He also said, "A man had two sons. [12] The younger of them said to his father, 'Father, give me the share of the estate I have coming to me.' So he distributed the assets to them. [13] Not many days later, the younger son gathered together all he had and traveled to a distant country, where he squandered his estate in foolish living. [14] After he had spent everything, a severe famine struck that country, and he had nothing. [15] Then he went to work for one of the citizens of that country, who sent him into his fields to feed pigs. [16] He longed to eat his fill from the pods that the pigs were eating, but no one would give him anything. [17] When he came to his senses, he said, 'How many of my father's hired workers have more than enough food, and here I am dying of hunger! [18] I'll get up, go to my father, and say to him, "Father, I have sinned against heaven and in your sight. [19] I'm no longer worthy to be called your son. Make me like one of your hired workers."' [20] So he got up and went to his father. But

QUESTIONS

What overall feeling does this story give you?

When the younger son asks for his portion of the estate, what is he asking for? When do sons typically receive this?

When the son received what he wanted, what does he do?

What trouble does the younger son run into while in a foreign land?

When he "hit rock bottom," what was he doing? Why was this significant to a Jewish audience?

Jesus says, "When he came to his senses." What does that mean?

What does the younger son decide to say to his father?

When the son returned to the father, what detail is given that allows us to see that the Father missed his son?

The son had a rehearsed speech. Was he able to recite it?

What blessings did the father give to his son when he returned?

What was the reaction of the household when the son returned?

What was the older brother doing when his younger brother returned?

What was his reaction when his younger brother returned? Why?

while the son was still a long way off, his father saw him and was filled with compassion. He ran, threw his arms around his neck, and kissed him. 21 The son said to him, 'Father, I have sinned against heaven and in your sight. I'm no longer worthy to be called your son.'

22 "But the father told his servants, 'Quick! Bring out the best robe and put it on him; put a ring on his finger and sandals on his feet. 23 Then bring the fattened calf and slaughter it, and let's celebrate with a feast, 24 because this son of mine was dead and is alive again; he was lost and is found!' So they began to celebrate.

25 "Now his older son was in the field; as he came near the house, he heard music and dancing. 26 So he summoned one of the servants, questioning what these things meant. 27 'Your brother is here,' he told him, 'and your father has slaughtered the fattened calf because he has him back safe and sound.'

28 "Then he became angry

and didn't want to go in. So his father came out and pleaded with him. ²⁹ But he replied to his father, 'Look, I have been slaving many years for you, and I have never disobeyed your orders, yet you never gave me a goat so that I could celebrate with my friends. ³⁰ But when this son of yours came, who has devoured your assets with prostitutes, you slaughtered the fattened calf for him.'

³¹ "'Son,' he said to him, 'you are always with me, and everything I have is yours. ³² But we had to celebrate and rejoice, because this brother of yours was dead and is alive again; he was lost and is found.'"

TEXT

QUESTIONS

Why did the older brother not want to go into the party?

What accusations did the older brother make against his brother?

What accusations did the older brother make against his father?

What was the father's response to the older son?

Was this similar to the response he had with his repentant son?

Which son is truly lost in this story?

This is the longest of Jesus's parables and probably most often explored because of the depth of its message. Most people tend to focus on the first part of the story. The prodigal son (prodigal means loose living and unwise spending) is the poster child for a sinner. He mistreats his father. He moves far away from where anyone knows him. He makes foolish decisions and backs himself into a hole financially. He becomes desperate, and then he decides to straighten his life. So many people can relate to this story of rebellion and repentance.

The older brother is also a lost son. While he is responsible and does not run away to live sinfully, he harbors hate and resentment. Like the younger son, he despises his father. He feels like a slave in his father's home. While the younger son repents, the older son does not and does not feel it necessary. He feels superior to his sinful brother.

Yet, both sons need to learn the same lesson. They were not in competition with each other. They should have been comparing themselves to the father, whose patience and love become the light of hope in the story. He readily accepted his son's repentance. He passionately pleaded with his older son to repent of his arrogance. His love for his children superseded any judgment or harsh treatment, although both deserved punishment. Love covers a multitude of sins (1 Pet 4.8).

Who is the bigger sinner? Who has bigger hurdles to overcome to be right with the father? Be ready to defend your answer.

If you were a Jew listening to this story, to what shocking moments would you have reacted?

The father is mistreated by both sons, yet he awaited the younger son's repentance and reassured his older son that all he had was his. What can we learn about God from the father in this story? What can we learn about how we should be ourselves?

Above all, maintain constant love for one another, since love covers a multitude of sins.

1 Peter 4.8

LOST COIN

Luke 15.8-10

Is there any context for this story? If so, what is it?

Who is speaking and to whom?

Are there other parables around this one or is this one on its own?

Identify where in Jesus's ministry you would place this parable and explain why.
   Beginning • Galilean Ministry • Judean Ministry • Final Weeks

Read the parable in two different translations and note any differences below.

⁸ "Or what woman who has ten silver coins, if she loses one coin, does not light a lamp, sweep the house, and search carefully until she finds it? ⁹ When she finds it, she calls her friends and neighbors together, saying, 'Rejoice with me, because I have found the silver coin I lost!' ¹⁰ I tell you, in the same way, there is joy in the presence of God's angels over one sinner who repents."

TEXT

QUESTIONS

What overall feeling does this story give you?

The woman has 10 silver coins. Why does she care about losing just one?

What does she do to find the coin?

When the finds the coin, who does she tell?

What is the reaction over finding the lost coin?

Jesus relates finding the lost coin to what spiritual event?

What happens in heaven when the lost is found?

Coins came in various values in the first century.

The shekel - is worth about two days' wages; The denarius - is worth about a full day's wage; the piece of silver - scholars disagree, from 5 - 120 days' wages; The talent - is a year of salary, to name a few.

We often wonder which type of coin this woman lost. Was it Jewish or Roman? Was it valuable or not valuable? We can make assumptions based on how she looked for the coin and how she rejoiced once she found it, but they are assumptions at best. What matters most in this parable is not the value of the coin but the value the woman places on the coin. She loses one of 10 and is willing to go to great lengths to find the one missing coin. She turns her house upside down, searching and cleaning.

Once she finds the coin, she is ecstatic—that is to be expected. But she also goes out and tells all of her neighbors. It is not hard to imagine that she also told them when she lost the coin so that they could rejoice with her when she found her missing treasure. This was a moment for celebration.

No matter the coin's value, we know that the value of a soul is immeasurable. If a woman and her neighbors rejoiced over something as simple as a coin, certainly, we can join the heavenly hosts to rejoice in a repentant soul.

Name something valuable you have lost. Tell the story.

Why do we not better keep track of things that we value? Why are we prone to lose things?

Imagine being the neighbors in this story. What would be your reaction?

How do we respond when someone repents?

"For they all gave out of their surplus, but she out of her poverty has put in everything she had — all she had to live on."

Mark 12.44

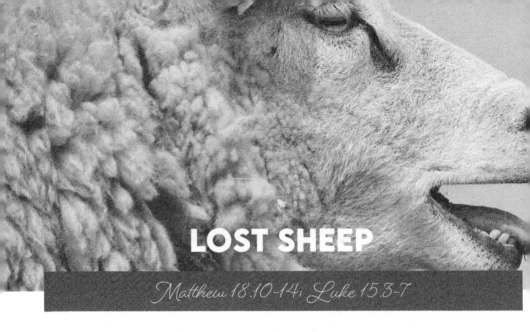

LOST SHEEP

Matthew 18:10-14; Luke 15:3-7

Is there any context for this story? If so, what is it?

Who is speaking and to whom?

Are there other parables around this one or is this one on its own?

Identify where in Jesus's ministry you would place this parable and explain why.
  Beginning • Galilean Ministry • Judean Ministry • Final Weeks

Read the parable in two different translations and note any differences below.

³ So he told them this parable: ⁴ "What man among you, who has a hundred sheep and loses one of them, does not leave the ninety-nine in the open field and go after the lost one until he finds it? ⁵ When he has found it, he joyfully puts it on his shoulders, ⁶ and coming home, he calls his friends and neighbors together, saying to them, 'Rejoice with me, because I have found my lost sheep!' ⁷ I tell you, in the same way, there will be more joy in heaven over one sinner who repents than over ninety-nine righteous people who don't need repentance.

What overall feeling does this story give you?

Name 5 other shepherds in Bible.

If the shepherd has 100 sheep, why does losing only one matter?

What does the shepherd do?

When he finds the sheep, what does he do?

How does finding the lost sheep make him feel?

What parallel happens in heaven when a sinner repents?

Luke 15 tells three parables, all of which clearly go together and reveal a similar truth—heaven rejoices when sinners repent.

Yet, the progression of the stories provides some interesting details. Note that the first story (Lost Sheep) is about one lost from 100. The second story (Lost Coin) is about one lost from 10. The last story is about one lost from two, but the twist is that both are lost.

Another progression is in value. A sheep has some value when sold at the market or when the wool becomes available. The coin potentially has more value. But who would value either over the value of one's child?

Jesus tells three related stories, but He raises the stakes in each story. He begins with the story of a desperate shepherd with a lost sheep. This is relatable in many ways compared to the role of shepherds throughout Scripture. We can think of those shepherds who led the flocks of God through Israel's history. Even the shepherds of God's flock today lead their sheep to spiritual food and drink. Shepherds are watchful protectors of their flocks.

No one is more watchful, loving, and providing than the Good Shepherd who watches over our souls — Jesus, who tells us this story. Indeed, He rejoices more than all when sinners repent.

Why do you think Jesus builds to the final parable in Luke 15? Who is he confronting in these parables, and about what?

Shepherds have a massive task to protect and provide for their flocks. What do we learn about shepherds from this parable?

How could we relate this to what we know about Jesus as the Chief Shepherd?

Acknowledge that the Lord is God.
He made us, and we are his—
his people, the sheep of his pasture.

Psalm 100.3

MASTER & SERVANT

Luke 17.7-10

Is there any context for this story? If so, what is it?

Who is speaking and to whom?

Are there other parables around this one or is this one on its own?

Identify where in Jesus's ministry you would place this parable and explain why.
  Beginning • Galilean Ministry • Judean Ministry • Final Weeks

Read the parable in two different translations and note any differences below.

TEXT

7 "Which one of you having a servant tending sheep or plowing will say to him when he comes in from the field, 'Come at once and sit down to eat'? 8 Instead, will he not tell him, 'Prepare something for me to eat, get ready, and serve me while I eat and drink; later you can eat and drink'? 9 Does he thank that servant because he did what was commanded? 10 In the same way, when you have done all that you were commanded, you should say, 'We are unworthy servants; we've only done our duty.'"

QUESTIONS

What overall feeling does this story give you?

What responsibilities does the servant have?

When the servant comes in from the field, is he mistreated? Explain your answer.

When does the servant get to relax and rest?

How does this relate to our relationship with God as our Master?

Does this parable match your current understanding of your relationship with God? Explain your answer.

We live in a society that wants to promote fairness and equality. We live with an ideal of freedom and talk often about rights and liberties. Our history has taught us to abhor slavery. We have watched people go on strike to gain more salary and benefits. Our country has a minimum wage, child labor laws, and other rules that prohibit the mistreatment of employees as much as possible.

Jesus's parable of the master and servant works against our sensibilities in some ways. These servants should be rewarded after toiling for so long in the hot sun. We think they deserve a break. Yet, Jesus uses the well-known concept of the first-century worker to express the idea of humility and servitude. He is less concerned about the worker's treatment than he is about the proper behavior of the worker. A good servant is not concerned with their ease. They are concerned about the needs and ease of their master. They will come inside and continue serving when they've finished their labor outside. The reason they give for this hard work is "duty." The motivation behind their duty is humility.

We often get fixated on what we want and forget to focus on what is proper. As the Preacher said, "God is in heaven and you are on earth" (Ecc 5.2). Let us serve until the Master is through with us.

Was the Master wrong for expecting the workers to serve him first?

Why would the servant consider themselves unworthy? How does this relate to our own relationship with the Master?

Do you think of God as a demanding Master or a loving Father? How does this parable alter your understanding of how we should view our relationship with God?

Do not be hasty to speak, and do not be impulsive to make a speech before God. God is in heaven and you are on earth, so let your words be few.

Ecclesiastes 5:2

MONEYLENDER

Luke 7:41-43

Is there any context for this story? If so, what is it?

Who is speaking and to whom?

Are there other parables around this one or is this one on its own?

Identify where in Jesus's ministry you would place this parable and explain why.
  Beginning • Galilean Ministry • Judean Ministry • Final Weeks

Read the parable in two different translations and note any differences below.

⁴¹ "A creditor had two debtors. One owed five hundred denarii, and the other fifty. ⁴² Since they could not pay it back, he graciously forgave them both. So, which of them will love him more?"

⁴³ Simon answered, "I suppose the one he forgave more."

"You have judged correctly," he told him.

What overall feeling does this story give you?

What did the creditor have owed to him?

Which person do you think felt more stress at their debt?

When these two were forgiven, how do you think they felt?

Which one will respond with more appreciation/love?

Simon gives the obvious answer. Looking at the context of this parable, how does this relate to Simon's own situation?

How should we view those "forgiven more?"

Forgiveness is special for both the giver and the receiver, and Jesus often spoke about its importance. He spoke of God's forgiveness of sinners and sinners forgiving sinners. He even went so far as to say that we should forgive seven times seventy times (Matt 18.21-22). This number implies that we are to forgive limitlessly.

While the parable Jesus tells in this context certainly speaks of forgiveness, it has less to do with our practice of forgiving others and more to do with our willingness to recognize their forgiveness. Jesus shows that those with more sins, baggage, and mistakes will be more appreciative and loving because of their forgiveness. Simon looked at the woman washing Jesus's feet with disdain and prejudice. Jesus was recognizing her greater love.

Often, even today, those of us who "have it together" and who have lived more faithfully will be tempted to look down on those who have made more mistakes. We should not. Those who have experienced greater forgiveness have the potential to be the most thankful and loving toward the God who has made them whole. Instead of seeing them as burdened with past mistakes, we should see them as finally unburdened and free to love our God again.

We do not know this woman's sins, other than she was called "a sinner." Simon judges Jesus by judging her as a "type of woman." You can hear the disdain dripping from his mouth as he speaks of her. No matter her sin, how should we view someone who is forgiven? How does this change our relationship with the forgiven?

If you had made some significant mistakes (and maybe you have), how can you feel towards a God who is willing to forgive?

How does being forgiven change you life?

If we confess our sins, he is faithful and just to forgive us our sins and to cleanse us from all unrighteousness.

1 John 1.9

MUSTARD SEED

Matthew 13.31-32; Mark 4.30-32; Luke 13.18-19

Is there any context for this story? If so, what is it?

Who is speaking and to whom?

Are there other parables around this one or is this one on its own?

Identify where in Jesus's ministry you would place this parable and explain why.
  Beginning • Galilean Ministry • Judean Ministry • Final Weeks

Read the parable in two different translations and note any differences below.

BEFORE YOU TACKLE THE TEXT

¹⁸ He said, therefore, "What is the kingdom of God like, and what can I compare it to? ¹⁹ It's like a mustard seed that a man took and sowed in his garden. It grew and became a tree, and the birds of the sky nested in its branches."

TEXT

QUESTIONS

What overall feeling does this story give you?

What is the "kingdom of God?"

What is signfiicant about a mustard seed?

How large can a mustard tree grow?

What does the tree make possible?

What other parables talk about the "growing" nature of the Kingdom?

If the Kingdom is supposed to grow, what does that require of us?

When we hear stories told in the New Testament, we should always consider the context of the entire Bible. Have these images and stories ever been told before in the Old Testament? Do similarities exist between Jesus's stories and ideas already familiar to the Jewish audience to whom Jesus was speaking?

The mustard seed growing into a large tree certainly has some parallels. Ezekiel speaks of a large tree growing when he speaks of Assyria (Eze 31.3-10). Nebuchadnezzar likewise dreams of a tree growing large enough that birds rest in its branches (Dan 4.10-12), and his tree represents his own kingdom of Babylon. Both of these trees are chopped down by judgment from God.

Ezekiel mentions another tree that grows large enough for birds to rest in its branches and is never chopped down in Ezekiel 17.22-24. This tree represents the kingdom of God. It is planted on Israel's high mountains. It will make all other trees look small in comparison. God says that He is powerful enough to bring down the tall tree and lift the short tree because this tree, representing His Kingdom, will prove that He is in control.

The Kingdom of God represents and proves God's reign on earth, and it will grow, expand, and spread until it provides rest.

There are multiple parables that mention the growth of God's Kingdom. Why does this matter to God?

If God is concerned with the growth of His Kingdom, and we care for the things of God, how can we help?

What holds us back from helping God's Kingdom grow?

"And I also say to you that
you are Peter, and on this rock
I will build my church, and
the gates of Hades will not
overpower it."

Matthew 16.18

NARROW DOOR

Luke 13.23-30

Is there any context for this story? If so, what is it?

Who is speaking and to whom?

Are there other parables around this one or is this one on its own?

Identify where in Jesus's ministry you would place this parable and explain why.

   Beginning • Galilean Ministry • Judean Ministry • Final Weeks

Read the parable in two different translations and note any differences below.

23 "Lord," someone asked him, "are only a few people going to be saved?"

He said to them, 24 "Make every effort to enter through the narrow door, because I tell you, many will try to enter and won't be able 25 once the homeowner gets up and shuts the door. Then you will stand outside and knock on the door, saying, 'Lord, open up for us!' He will answer you, 'I don't know you or where you're from.' 26 Then you will say, 'We ate and drank in your presence, and you taught in our streets.' 27 But he will say, 'I tell you, I don't know you or where you're from. Get away from me, all you evildoers!' 28 There will be weeping and gnashing of teeth in that place, when you see Abraham, Isaac, Jacob, and all the prophets in the kingdom of God, but yourselves thrown out. 29 They will come from east and west, from north and south, to share the banquet in the kingdom of God. 30 Note this: Some who are last will be first, and some who are first will be last."

TEXT

QUESTIONS

What overall feeling does this story give you?

What is the concern the questioner has?

How does Jesus describe the entrance to the Kingdom of God?

What happens if the master shuts the door?

What arguments will people make to try and get the master to open the door?

What will the master say to those on the outside?

What will cause great mourning?

No one likes to be excluded. Yet, many will be excluded from the Kingdom of God for no reason other than they decided to stay on the outside. While the context of this parable likely refers to those Jewish leaders who refused to come to the Kingdom as Jesus taught it, there is a similar warning for us today if we decide that we would rather stay in the world than go into the Kingdom of God. At some point, we will realize the value of being in God's Kingdom and want in.

But what if it is too late? What excuses can we use to convince God that we belong inside when the door is shut? There is no good reason to stay outside of God's Kingdom. Certainly, there are many selfish reasons: we want to have fun, we want our way, we want more of the world, etc. But there are no good reasons.

You have been invited into the Kingdom of God. He wants all to be saved (1 Tim 2.4), and He has done what is necessary to give you that chance (Tit 2.11). But He will not force anyone through the door of the Kingdom. And there is coming a time when entrance into the Kingdom will be closed off. Those who enter the door will experience eternal joy, and those who refuse to enter the door will be eternally rejected.

No one likes to be excluded, so God invites all. Will you walk through that door He holds open for you?

What other times has Jesus talked about doors? Give references.

Why would Jesus exclude anyone? Why would He not let them in late?

This parable creates a sense of urgency. What is it urging you personally to do in your life?

How narrow is the gate and difficult the road that leads to life, and few find it.

Matthew 7.14

NEW CLOTH & WINESKIN

Matthew 9.16-17; Mark 2.21-22; Luke 5.36-38

Is there any context for this story? If so, what is it?

Who is speaking and to whom?

Are there other parables around this one or is this one on its own?

Identify where in Jesus's ministry you would place this parable and explain why.
   Beginning • Galilean Ministry • Judean Ministry • Final Weeks

Read the parable in two different translations and note any differences below.

¹⁴ Then John's disciples came to him, saying, "Why do we and the Pharisees fast often, but your disciples do not fast?"

¹⁵ Jesus said to them, "Can the wedding guests be sad while the groom is with them? The time will come when the groom will be taken away from them, and then they will fast. ¹⁶ No one patches an old garment with unshrunk cloth, because the patch pulls away from the garment and makes the tear worse. ¹⁷ And no one puts new wine into old wineskins. Otherwise, the skins burst, the wine spills out, and the skins are ruined. No, they put new wine into fresh wineskins, and both are preserved."

TEXT

QUESTIONS

What overall feeling does this story give you?

Jesus was accused of not having his disciples fast. What was his reason for this?

While the groom is present, what should be the mood? What about when the groom leaves?

Why does new cloth not belong on old cloth?

Why does not wine not belong in old wineskins?

What similarities exist between these two illustrations? What differences?

What do these parables have to do with the presence of the "groom?"

These parables seemingly do not belong in their context. What do a patch of cloth and a wineskin have to do with the presence of a groom? This question forces us to think a little deeper about what is happening in the story.

Jesus is teaching contrasts or things that do not belong together. First, mourning and fasting do not belong with times of celebration. Second, new, unshrunk cloth belongs on something other than old fabric. Third, new wine, which will ferment and put off gas, belongs in something other than old wineskins which will crack and burst instead of expand with the fermenting new wine. In Luke, Jesus adds, "And no one, after drinking old wine, wants new, because he says, 'The old is better'" (5.39).

All three of these illustrations explained an important principle to John's disciples, who were asking him questions. The complaint is that Jesus is not doing things properly because His disciples are not acting somber or stoic enough. They are not taking their faith seriously.

Jesus is helping them to understand the issue. He is saying that new things sometimes do not mix with old things. Instead, we must keep things in their proper places. For the disciples, who have realized that they have the Messiah, it is time for joy and celebration, but He also hints that a time is coming for sadness. Instead of mixing the new with the old, they must appreciate each thing in its proper place.

ADDITIONAL THOUGHTS

What new things was Jesus doing that would have confused those who were wanting things to be done by tradition or the old ways?

How did Jesus often respond to the Pharisees who were more concerned about their tradition than God's Law? Give some examples.

Is Jesus teaching that new things are better than old things? Defend your answer.

THOUGHT QUESTIONS

"...take off your former way of life,
the old self that is corrupted by
deceitful desires, to be renewed in
the spirit of your minds, and to put
on the new self,

Ephesians 4.21-23

PERSISTENT WIDOW

Luke 18.1-8

Is there any context for this story? If so, what is it?

Who is speaking and to whom?

Are there other parables around this one or is this one on its own?

Identify where in Jesus's ministry you would place this parable and explain why.
   Beginning • Galilean Ministry • Judean Ministry • Final Weeks

Read the parable in two different translations and note any differences below.

¹ Now he told them a parable on the need for them to pray always and not give up. ² "There was a judge in a certain town who didn't fear God or respect people. ³ And a widow in that town kept coming to him, saying, 'Give me justice against my adversary.'

⁴ "For a while he was unwilling, but later he said to himself, 'Even though I don't fear God or respect people, ⁵ yet because this widow keeps pestering me, I will give her justice, so that she doesn't wear me out by her persistent coming.'"

⁶ Then the Lord said, "Listen to what the unjust judge says. ⁷ Will not God grant justice to his elect who cry out to him day and night? Will he delay helping them? ⁸ I tell you that he will swiftly grant them justice. Nevertheless, when the Son of Man comes, will he find faith on earth?"

QUESTIONS

What overall feeling does this story give you?

What topic does Luke tell us Jesus was teaching about?

How is the judge described?

What did the widow demand?

Why would the judge not help?

Why did the judge finally help?

How is God like this judge?

How is God not like this judge?

The parables typically have a pattern where the master, father, or ruler in the story references God. We, therefore, expect masters who rule fairly and fathers who act lovingly.

In this parable, the judge is unfair and harsh. He only helps when he is worn out, and he only acts with compassion when he feels forced. In the story, he seems to know the proper judgment, but he refuses to give it. Or maybe he cares little about the appropriate judgment and gives the widow what she asks for regardless. The whole story shines a negative light on the judge, which becomes surprising when Jesus compares this judge to His Father.

The story clearly does not intend to represent the Father in character but to offer reassurance that if an unrighteous judge can do the right thing through continued petition, certainly a righteous God who is generous will eventually answer the petitions of His people.

That petition, though, is interesting in itself. This is not a parable about begging God for whatever trinket or prize you want. Instead, it was an answer to a specific problem. The abused and persecuted saints wish for justice, and they know that it only comes from God. Jesus clearly says they should never give up and surrender to the world. God is just. God will redeem and avenge His people. God will make wrong things right.

What injustices do Christians face in the world today? Have you personally suffered because of belonging to Christ?

When have you prayed continually for the solution to a problem that only God could solve? How did this turn out?

If we are to pray for justice, what does this require from us as followers of Jesus? How should we live?

Therefore the Lord is waiting to show you mercy,
and is rising up to show you compassion,
for the Lord is a just God.
All who wait patiently for him are happy.

Isaiah 30.18

PHARISEE & TAX COLLECTOR

Luke 18:10-14

Is there any context for this story? If so, what is it?

Who is speaking and to whom?

Are there other parables around this one or is this one on its own?

Identify where in Jesus's ministry you would place this parable and explain why.
    Beginning • Galilean Ministry • Judean Ministry • Final Weeks

Read the parable in two different translations and note any differences below.

⁹ He also told this parable to some who trusted in themselves that they were righteous and looked down on everyone else: ¹⁰ "Two men went up to the temple to pray, one a Pharisee and the other a tax collector. ¹¹ The Pharisee was standing and praying like this about himself: 'God, I thank you that I'm not like other people—greedy, unrighteous, adulterers, or even like this tax collector. ¹² I fast twice a week; I give a tenth of everything I get.'

¹³ "But the tax collector, standing far off, would not even raise his eyes to heaven but kept striking his chest and saying, 'God, have mercy on me, a sinner!' ¹⁴ I tell you, this one went down to his house justified rather than the other, because everyone who exalts himself will be humbled, but the one who humbles himself will be exalted."

TEXT QUESTIONS

What overall feeling does this story give you?

Two men prayed. Name what made them different.

What is a Pharisee?

What is your perception of the Pharisee?

What is a tax collector?

What is your perception of the tax collector?

Who was justified by God? Why?

How can we be more like the one who was justified?

Pharisees were the righteous of the righteous. This is made clear when Jesus taught that righteousness had to exceed the Pharisees and scribes as if that were a high bar (Matt 5.20). The standard that this Pharisee bragged about was not unrealistic:

He fasted twice a week—the Jewish Law commanded several fasts.

He gave a tenth—this is often called the tithe. This man was sure he gave a tenth, not just of his profit. He gave a tithe of everything.

The problem with this Pharisee is that he had a high view of himself. He was not "greedy," "unrighteous," or an "adulterer." Then, he even had a low view of others, calling out the tax collector nearby.

When Jewish audiences heard this parable, they likely accepted it as a real scenario. The Pharisees were pompous, often comparing themselves to others so they might feel good about their righteousness. Jesus later calls them "white-washed tombs" (Matt 23.27). He says they were filthy cups with only the outside cleaned (23.25). This means they looked good from the outside, but the inside was dead and dirty.

In Matthew 23.23, Jesus says they should have tithed, as this Pharisee boasted, but they should have done so without neglecting the more important matters of the Law ("justice, mercy, and faithfulness"). In this parable, the Pharisees clearly had no view of compassion and humility.

Why did the Pharisee see himself so exalted? Do Christians struggle with this today?

Why did the tax collector see himself so humbly? Do Christians struggle with this today?

How should we view ourselves? To whom should we compare ourselves? Explain.

Don't store up for yourselves treasures on earth, where moth and rust destroy and where thieves break in and steal. But store up for yourselves treasures in heaven, where neither moth nor rust destroys, and where thieves don't break in and steal. For where your treasure is, there your heart will be also.

Matthew 6.19-21

PLACE OF HONOR

Luke 14.7-11

Is there any context for this story? If so, what is it?

Who is speaking and to whom?

Are there other parables around this one or is this one on its own?

Identify where in Jesus's ministry you would place this parable and explain why.
   Beginning • Galilean Ministry • Judean Ministry • Final Weeks

Read the parable in two different translations and note any differences below.

7 He told a parable to those who were invited, when he noticed how they would choose the best places for themselves: 8 "When you are invited by someone to a wedding banquet, don't sit in the place of honor, because a more distinguished person than you may have been invited by your host. 9 The one who invited both of you may come and say to you, 'Give your place to this man,' and then in humiliation, you will proceed to take the lowest place.

10 "But when you are invited, go and sit in the lowest place, so that when the one who invited you comes, he will say to you, 'Friend, move up higher.' You will then be honored in the presence of all the other guests. 11 For everyone who exalts himself will be humbled, and the one who humbles himself will be exalted."

What overall feeling does this story give you?

What bad behavior does Jesus address in this parable?

Is this merely a parable or has Jesus observed the behavior He speaks of?

What advice does Jesus give to those attending the banquet?

Why does this advice make sense?

What is the key characteristic to the proper social mores?

Do you think Jesus is more concerned with their character or their ability to be socially exalted?

Embarrassment comes to all at some point. We've all misspoke, accidentally mixed people up, or done something we later regret. We even have nightmares about appearing in public and being embarrassed. We get red-faced whenever we even think about those moments.

Jesus uses our aversion to embarrassment to teach an important lesson—humility—while observing the poor choices of those attending the meal. They were choosing the best seats reserved for the most important guests at the risk of being moved away from the host to places of less honor. Jesus's logic is that they should move away from the host to be called to a better place at the table publicly.

This is Proverbs 29.23 in action: "A person's pride will humble him, but a humble spirit will gain honor." Jesus shows that others will praise those willing to be humble. As another proverb says, "Let another praise you, and not your own mouth—a stranger, and not your own lips" (27.2). Instead of talking about our honor or acting as if we are something big, we should let others praise us.

This does require that we be someone worth praising. We must work hard, live righteously, and have the kind of character that people want to praise.

What kind of person gets praised?

What kind of work gets praised?

What kind of person is rejected?

Can you think of any verses that help us learn how we can be more worthy of honor?

*Let another praise you, and not
your own mouth—
a stranger, and not your own lips.*

Proverbs 27.2

RETURNING OWNER

Mark 13:34-37

Is there any context for this story? If so, what is it?

Who is speaking and to whom?

Are there other parables around this one or is this one on its own?

Identify where in Jesus's ministry you would place this parable and explain why.

Beginning • Galilean Ministry • Judean Ministry • Final Weeks

Read the parable in two different translations and note any differences below.

³⁴ "It is like a man on a journey, who left his house, gave authority to his servants, gave each one his work, and commanded the doorkeeper to be alert. ³⁵ Therefore be alert, since you don't know when the master of the house is coming— whether in the evening or at midnight or at the crowing of the rooster or early in the morning. ³⁶ Otherwise, when he comes suddenly he might find you sleeping. ³⁷ And what I say to you, I say to everyone: Be alert!"

What overall feeling does this story give you?

Why did the man have to leave?

What does it mean that he "gave authority to his servants?"

Jesus jumps straight into application. What is that application?

Can you find other verses in the Bible that have the same application?

What does it mean to be alert?

Why is alertness necessary?

Jesus often talked about alertness, and several of His parables address this theme. He was concerned that when disaster strikes or when the Lord returns, those who belong to him are alert.

Ultimately, the idea of alertness branches into the concept of preparedness. How can you be alert for something when you do not know when it will happen? You stay prepared. How do slaves stand alert at their master's return when they do not know when he is coming? They remain at the door prepared. How do people stay prepared for the possibility of thieves? They set up security and remain prepared.

For Christians today, we are expected to remain prepared and alert for two things: the temptation for sin and the coming of our Master. We must remain vigilant against temptation. We must realize that the devil is prowling around, seeking those we can devour (1 Pet 5.8). We must take temptations seriously and avoid failing (Jam 1.12). Those who remain alert will succeed (1 Cor 16.13-14).

Likewise, we must remain alert for Jesus's return, not out of fear of being caught unaware but in anticipation that the One we love has come again. We eagerly anticipate His return (Heb 9.28), which we can only do if we are confident that He will find us faithful. We must live righteous lives and be busy about His work, as dutiful servants serving their master until He returns.

How do alert people respond in danger? How do those who are unaware respond?

What dangers do we face? How can remaining alert help us through temptations we face? Give specific examples.

Do you look forward to the return of Jesus? Why or why not? What is necessary for your to anticipate the end of life or the end of the world?

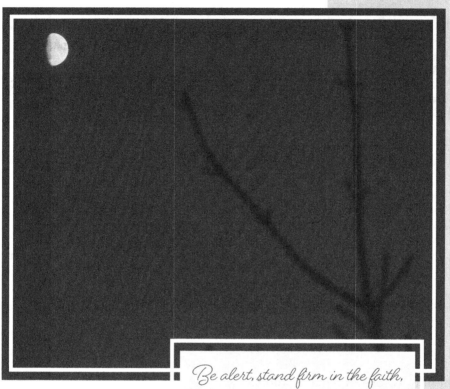

Be alert, stand firm in the faith, be courageous, be strong. Do everything in love.

1 Corinthians 16.13-14

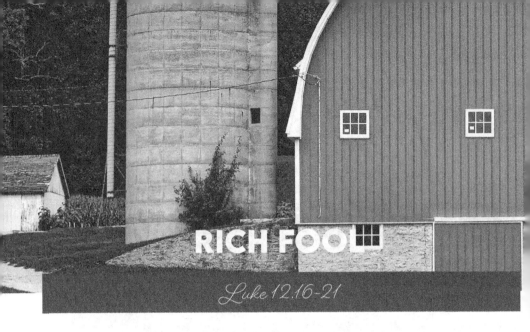

RICH FOOL

Luke 12:16-21

Is there any context for this story? If so, what is it?

Who is speaking and to whom?

Are there other parables around this one or is this one on its own?

Identify where in Jesus's ministry you would place this parable and explain why.
Beginning • Galilean Ministry • Judean Ministry • Final Weeks

Read the parable in two different translations and note any differences below.

16 Then he told them a parable: "A rich man's land was very productive. 17 He thought to himself, 'What should I do, since I don't have anywhere to store my crops? 18 I will do this,' he said. 'I'll tear down my barns and build bigger ones and store all my grain and my goods there. 19 Then I'll say to myself, "You have many goods stored up for many years. Take it easy; eat, drink, and enjoy yourself."'

20 "But God said to him, 'You fool! This very night your life is demanded of you. And the things you have prepared—whose will they be?'

21 "That's how it is with the one who stores up treasure for himself and is not rich toward God."

QUESTIONS

What overall feeling does this story give you?

The man in this story is rich. Is that good or bad?

What does this man do with his surplus of crops?

Does this man's actions make sense? Explain.

What will this man do now that he has a surplus of goods?

What does God call him and why?

What is the problem with stored up riches once someone dies?

What is the real problem with this man according to verse 21?

Over the years, many people have taught that being rich is wrong. Jesus taught that it was difficult for a rich man to go to heaven (Matt 19.23-24). Jesus often uses rich people as fools in his stories. Yet, the problem is not their riches. If so, then Abraham, David, Solomon, and others would have been condemned for their wealth.

Instead, Jesus is using rich people to thwart the expectations of the crowds. There was an understanding in the first century that rich people were rich because God was pleased with them, and poor people were displeasing to God. Jesus is showing that this is often not the case. Rich people tend to put their trust in riches, and poor people tend to steal to make ends meet (cf. Pro 30.7-9). The issue is not the amount of money in a bank account but, as Jesus points out at the end of this parable, how much treasure they have placed in God. Like Jesus says, "For where your treasure is, there will your heart be also" (Matt 6.21). Jesus teaches that our hearts, treasures, actions, thoughts, words, relationships, and all else belong to God. Instead of building barns to provide for earthly wealth and sitting back to do nothing, we should lay up treasures in heaven, focusing on those things that matter eternally.

For the rich, we are instructed to do good "that they may take hold of that life that is truly life" (1 Tim 6.17-19).

Is it wrong to enjoy ease of life? Is it wrong to retire and enjoy the fruits of your labor? Explain and give verses to support your answer.

How much attention do you put into the "treasures of earth" versus the "treasures of heaven?" Consider hours devoted to work and education, devoted attention, and stress.

Using 1 Tim 6.17-19, make a list of things we should be doing with our money to lay up treasures in heaven.

Instruct those who are rich in the present age not to be arrogant or to set their hope on the uncertainty of wealth, but on God, who richly provides us with all things to enjoy.

1 Timothy 6.9

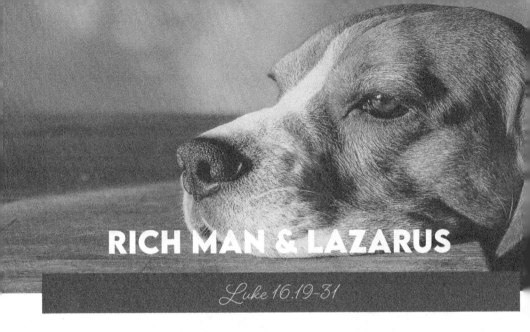

RICH MAN & LAZARUS

Luke 16.19-31

Is there any context for this story? If so, what is it?

Who is speaking and to whom?

Are there other parables around this one or is this one on its own?

Identify where in Jesus's ministry you would place this parable and explain why.
  Beginning • Galilean Ministry • Judean Ministry • Final Weeks

Read the parable in two different translations and note any differences below.

¹⁹ "There was a rich man who would dress in purple and fine linen, feasting lavishly every day. ²⁰ But a poor man named Lazarus, covered with sores, was lying at his gate. ²¹ He longed to be filled with what fell from the rich man's table, but instead the dogs would come and lick his sores. ²² One day the poor man died and was carried away by the angels to Abraham's side. The rich man also died and was buried. ²³ And being in torment in Hades, he looked up and saw Abraham a long way off, with Lazarus at his side. ²⁴ 'Father Abraham!' he called out, 'Have mercy on me and send Lazarus to dip the tip of his finger in water and cool my tongue, because I am in agony in this flame!'

²⁵ "'Son,' Abraham said, 'remember that during your life you received your good things, just as Lazarus received bad things, but now he is comforted here, while you are in agony. ²⁶ Besides all this, a great chasm has been fixed between us and you, so that those who

TEXT

QUESTIONS

What overall feeling does this story give you?

What is the name of the rich man? What is the name of the poor man?

How is the poor man described?

When the poor man dies, what intersting things happens?

When the rich man dies, what happens?

Where does the rich man go?

Where does the poor man go?

What experience does the rich man have after death?

Why can the rich man not get to where the poor man is?

What does the rich man first ask for? What answer does he receive?

What does the rich man ask for next? What answer does he receive?

What does this mean for us as we live this life? How should we find the best destiny after this life?

want to pass over from here to you cannot; neither can those from there cross over to us.'

27 "'Father,' he said, 'then I beg you to send him to my father's house— 28 because I have five brothers—to warn them, so that they won't also come to this place of torment.'

29 "But Abraham said, 'They have Moses and the prophets; they should listen to them.'

30 "'No, father Abraham,' he said. 'But if someone from the dead goes to them, they will repent.'

31 "But he told him, 'If they don't listen to Moses and the prophets, they will not be persuaded if someone rises from the dead.'"

Many have surmised that this is not a parable but a real story, considering Jesus names Lazarus (and never names a character in any other parable). While we cannot know for sure, we can understand that Jesus's parables often describe real life, and this description of life after death might well depict reality.

If that is the case, immediately upon death, some go to a place of comfort, and some go to a place of torment. There is no clue about the difference between these two men other than their wealth and comfort in life. Not much can be concluded based on such limited information. Interestingly, Abraham tells the rich man that those who want to avoid the torment of the afterlife should listen to Moses and the prophets (the Scriptures) and that even a resurrected person could not convince those who do not want to repent. Something about the rich man's life needed repentance.

Because we know so little about Lazarus, we cannot conclude much about morality as much as the need to make the right choices now. Neither Lazarus nor the rich man seemed to expect to die, but both did. One was prepared. One was not.

In this parable, Jesus makes it clear that we should build our lives in a way that prepares us for the outcome we want. If we want to rest with the faithful, we must live faithfully.

When were these men judged to see their respective places as their destiny?

What is the rich man's greatest concern during his suffering?

What does the Bible teach about hell and heaven? Give some verses to support your answers.

SHEEP & GOATS

Matthew 25.31-46

Is there any context for this story? If so, what is it?

Who is speaking and to whom?

Are there other parables around this one or is this one on its own?

Identify where in Jesus's ministry you would place this parable and explain why.
   Beginning • Galilean Ministry • Judean Ministry • Final Weeks

Read the parable in two different translations and note any differences below.

31 "When the Son of Man comes in his glory, and all the angels with him, then he will sit on his glorious throne. 32 All the nations will be gathered before him, and he will separate them one from another, just as a shepherd separates the sheep from the goats. 33 He will put the sheep on his right and the goats on the left. 34 Then the King will say to those on his right, 'Come, you who are blessed by my Father; inherit the kingdom prepared for you from the foundation of the world.

35 "'For I was hungry and you gave me something to eat; I was thirsty and you gave me something to drink; I was a stranger and you took me in; 36 I was naked and you clothed me; I was sick and you took care of me; I was in prison and you visited me.'

37 "Then the righteous will answer him, 'Lord, when did we see you hungry and feed you, or thirsty and give you something to drink? 38 When did we see you a stranger and take you in, or without clothes and clothe you? 39 When did we see you sick, or in prison, and visit you?'

TEXT QUESTIONS

What overall feeling does this story give you?

Who will be gathered before the Son of Man?

Who is the Son of Man?

People are compared to what animals in this teaching? Which are righteous and which are wicked?

Which animals will be placed where before the King?

What six negative conditions did the King say he experienced?

What did the sheep do?

What confused the sheep?

117

What did the goats do for the King's needs?

What confused the goats?

What did the King say would happen to the goats?

For whom is the eternal fire prepared for?

How did the King say they did or did not serve him?

Who gets eternal life? Who gets eternal punishment?

40 "And the King will answer them, 'Truly I tell you, whatever you did for one of the least of these brothers and sisters of mine, you did for me.'

41 "Then he will also say to those on the left, 'Depart from me, you who are cursed, into the eternal fire prepared for the devil and his angels! 42 For I was hungry and you gave me nothing to eat; I was thirsty and you gave me nothing to drink; 43 I was a stranger and you didn't take me in; I was naked and you didn't clothe me, sick and in prison and you didn't take care of me.'

44 "Then they too will answer, 'Lord, when did we see you hungry, or thirsty, or a stranger, or without clothes, or sick, or in prison, and not help you?'

45 "Then he will answer them, 'Truly I tell you, whatever you did not do for one of the least of these, you did not do for me.'

46 "And they will go away into eternal punishment, but the righteous into eternal life."

God's creation has always been given a choice. From the first days of the Garden of Eden, Adam and Eve were told to choose between a tree that brought life and a tree that brought death. They were to choose between God's way and their own way. These same options have presented themselves in various ways throughout history.

The Bible also discusses two choices by describing two groups: light versus dark, sheep and goats, and new versus old. Repeatedly, people are placed on one side or the other and called to choose which side they want to be on. Joshua tells the people to choose this day who they would serve (Jos 24.15). Elijah challenges the people to choose between Baal and God (1 Kin 18.21-22).

Jesus again lays that choice out for us in this parable. We can be righteous or unrighteous, sheep or goats. Ultimately, the choices we make show whether we want to be part of God's kingdom or not. We are choosing, every day, in every action, in every decision, whether we serve the King or not.

Although Jesus does not directly call us to choose as Joshua did, he does indirectly. Jesus wants us to serve God by serving "the least of these." What qualifies someone as the least? It seems that it is the hungry, thirsty, imprisoned stranger. We serve the forgotten because the King has not forgotten them.

How do we care for the hungry, thirsty, stranger...?

When we do this, who are we really serving?

Does this parable teach that we act so that we might earn salvation or eternal life? Explain your answer.

SHREWD MANAGER

Luke 16:1-9

Is there any context for this story? If so, what is it?

Who is speaking and to whom?

Are there other parables around this one or is this one on its own?

Identify where in Jesus's ministry you would place this parable and explain why.
   Beginning • Galilean Ministry • Judean Ministry • Final Weeks

Read the parable in two different translations and note any differences below.

¹ Now he said to the disciples, "There was a rich man who received an accusation that his manager was squandering his possessions. ² So he called the manager in and asked, 'What is this I hear about you? Give an account of your management, because you can no longer be my manager.'

³ "Then the manager said to himself, 'What will I do since my master is taking the management away from me? I'm not strong enough to dig; I'm ashamed to beg. ⁴ I know what I'll do so that when I'm removed from management, people will welcome me into their homes.'

⁵ "So he summoned each one of his master's debtors. 'How much do you owe my master?' he asked the first one.

⁶ "'A hundred measures of olive oil,' he said.

"'Take your invoice,' he told him, 'sit down quickly, and write fifty.'

⁷ "Next he asked another,

What overall feeling does this story give you?

This story involves a rich man and a manager. What do we learn about the manager?

Why does the rich man call the manager to give an account?

How does the manager handle this request?

What limitations does the manager put on himself? Do you think these are true?

Is the manager honest or not in the way he is working?

What motivation does the manager have in doing what he does?

As the manager starts bringing in money, how does the rich man respond?

The manager is said to act "shrewdly." What does this word mean?

Jesus's explanation following the story is hard to understand. What do you think Jesus means in verse 8-9?

Those faithful in little can be trusted with what?

Those faithful with much can be trusted with what?

Give your own interpretation of this parable.

'How much do you owe?'

"'A hundred measures of wheat,' he said.

"'Take your invoice,' he told him, 'and write eighty.'

8 "The master praised the unrighteous manager because he had acted shrewdly. For the children of this age are more shrewd than the children of light in dealing with their own people. 9 And I tell you, make friends for yourselves by means of worldly wealth so that when it fails, they may welcome you into eternal dwellings. 10 Whoever is faithful in very little is also faithful in much, and whoever is unrighteous in very little is also unrighteous in much. 11 So if you have not been faithful with worldly wealth, who will trust you with what is genuine? 12 And if you have not been faithful with what belongs to someone else, who will give you what is your own?

Of all of the parables, this one confuses people the most. How could Jesus commend someone who acted shrewdly? How could Jesus admire dishonesty?

The key to understanding this parable is found in Jesus's explanation. He describes how the world works in this parable, not the Kingdom. He shows that "children of this age," meaning those who belong to the world, are more shrewd than the "children of light," or those belonging to the Kingdom. The world is better at handling the world, which makes sense. Worldly people understand worldly people. Those who make friends with those of the world will be welcomed into eternal dwellings, meaning the eternal dwellings in which the worldly people dwell. In a twist of concepts, Jesus uses eternal dwellings to refer to everlasting punishment in this case.

To reinforce this explanation, Jesus teaches that unfaithfulness is rewarded with little trust, and faithfulness is rewarded with abundant trust. He also explains that if we can be trusted with small things like money (what is worldly), then we can be better trusted with genuine things (what is spiritual).

Jesus is not promoting trickery and dishonesty but using shrewdness as an example to show that worldliness brings about worldly results. In contrast, genuineness and honesty bring about eternal good.

Do you find it hard to think through this parable? Explain why.

If you were to rewrite this parable in a simpler form, how would you rewrite it?

Consider the next verse (Luke 16.13). How does this relate to the parable and broaden our understanding?

SOWER

Matthew 13.2-23; Mark 4.3-20; Luke 8.5-15

Is there any context for this story? If so, what is it?

Who is speaking and to whom?

Are there other parables around this one or is this one on its own?

Identify where in Jesus's ministry you would place this parable and explain why.

   Beginning • Galilean Ministry • Judean Ministry • Final Weeks

Read the parable in two different translations and note any differences below.

5 "A sower went out to sow his seed. As he sowed, some seed fell along the path; it was trampled on, and the birds of the sky devoured it. 6 Other seed fell on the rock; when it grew up, it withered away, since it lacked moisture. 7 Other seed fell among thorns; the thorns grew up with it and choked it. 8 Still other seed fell on good ground; when it grew up, it produced fruit: a hundred times what was sown." As he said this, he called out, "Let anyone who has ears to hear listen."

9 Then his disciples asked him, "What does this parable mean?" 10 So he said, "The secrets of the kingdom of God have been given for you to know, but to the rest it is in parables, so that

Looking they may not see, and hearing they may not understand.

11 "This is the meaning of the parable: The seed is the word of God. 12 The seed along the path are those who have heard and then the devil comes and takes away the word from their hearts, so that

TEXT

QUESTIONS

What overall feeling does this story give you?

The seed landed on four different types of soil. What were these four?

What happened to the seed in the first type of soil?

What happened to the seed in the second type of soil?

What happened to the seed in the third type of soil?

What happened to the seed in the fourth type of soil?

How much fruit was produced?

What was the reason Jesus told parables?

When Jesus explained the parable to the disciples, what did the path represent?

What did the rocky soil represent?

What did the thorny soil represent?

What did the good soil represent?

Why should we desire to "produce fruit?"

they may not believe and be saved. 13 And the seed on the rock are those who, when they hear, receive the word with joy. Having no root, these believe for a while and fall away in a time of testing. 14 As for the seed that fell among thorns, these are the ones who, when they have heard, go on their way and are choked with worries, riches, and pleasures of life, and produce no mature fruit. 15 But the seed in the good ground— these are the ones who, having heard the word with an honest and good heart, hold on to it and by enduring, produce fruit.

Parables do not often come with their own cheat sheet, but Jesus gives us exactly that with the Sower. This allows us to know for certain that we are interpreting this parable as Jesus intended it to be understood. This parable is appropriately explained because it reveals a truth that we face when coming to the parable. We get to decide how we are going to hear Jesus's teachings.

Will we be the pathway, hardened and unfruitful? Will we let Jesus's teachings just bounce off of us? Will we ignore them? Will we hear them but never let them root into our lives? Will we let distractions choke out Jesus's words?

Hopefully, we intend to avoid all of those descriptions. Instead, we want Jesus's teachings to sink into our hearts, take deep root, and produce much fruit. If we hear the value of Jesus's words, we should know that they can change us, mold us, and cause us to be productive in His Kingdom. We will develop our character in a way that allows Jesus's words to produce fruit.

What's interesting about this illustration is that no one ever pays attention to the dirt of a productive field. They notice the healthy plants and abundant fruit and imagine the harvest to come. They praise the farmer for his skill in growing such lovely crops. In our own case, we must live in a way that brings attention to the farmer (cf. Matt 5.16).

While type of soil are you? Explain.

Can we change what type of soil we are?

How does God's Word take root?

What do fruits look like for Christians?

TALENTS

Matthew 25.14-30; Luke 19.12-27

Is there any context for this story? If so, what is it?

Who is speaking and to whom?

Are there other parables around this one or is this one on its own?

Identify where in Jesus's ministry you would place this parable and explain why.

   Beginning • Galilean Ministry • Judean Ministry • Final Weeks

Read the parable in two different translations and note any differences below.

14 "For it is just like a man about to go on a journey. He called his own servants and entrusted his possessions to them. 15 To one he gave five talents, to another two talents, and to another one talent, depending on each one's ability. Then he went on a journey. Immediately 16 the man who had received five talents went, put them to work, and earned five more. 17 In the same way the man with two earned two more. 18 But the man who had received one talent went off, dug a hole in the ground, and hid his master's money.

19 "After a long time the master of those servants came and settled accounts with them. 20 The man who had received five talents approached, presented five more talents, and said, 'Master, you gave me five talents. See, I've earned five more talents.'

21 "His master said to him, 'Well done, good and faithful servant! You were faithful over a few things; I will put you in charge of many things. Share your master's joy.'

22 "The man with two talents also approached. He said, 'Master, you gave me two talents. See, I've earned two more talents.'

23 "His master said to him,

TEXT QUESTIONS

What overall feeling does this story give you?

What is a "talent" in this story?

How much did he give the first servant?

What did that servant do with the money?

How much did he give the second servant?

What did that servant do with the money?

How much did he give the third servant?

What did that servant do with the money?

QUESTIONS

Which servants pleased the master?

Which servant did not please the master?

What reason did the master give for his displeasure?

What did the master say the servant should have done?

What happened to the bad servant's talent?

What happened to the bad servant?

TEXT

'Well done, good and faithful servant! You were faithful over a few things; I will put you in charge of many things. Share your master's joy.'

24 "The man who had received one talent also approached and said, 'Master, I know you. You're a harsh man, reaping where you haven't sown and gathering where you haven't scattered seed. 25 So I was afraid and went off and hid your talent in the ground. See, you have what is yours.'

26 "His master replied to him, 'You evil, lazy servant! If you knew that I reap where I haven't sown and gather where I haven't scattered, 27 then you should have deposited my money with the bankers, and I would have received my money back with interest when I returned.

28 "'So take the talent from him and give it to the one who has ten talents. 29 For to everyone who has, more will be given, and he will have more than enough. But from the one who does not have, even what he has will be taken away from him. 30 And throw this good-for-nothing servant into the outer darkness, where there will be weeping and gnashing of teeth.'

This parable often confuses people because it uses the word "talent." Because that word means "skills or abilities" in our modern language, it is assumed that this is the point of the parable. This is unlikely.

But this parable is about something other than money management, too. Talents, a measure of money in the Roman world, were distributed among some servants, and they were expected to produce good results through these resources. Two of the servants do as expected and do it well. They double the master's resources, prove themselves trustworthy and capable, and the master rewards them with continued trust. They are allowed to continue their work. The third does not. He hides the money. He does nothing. He does not lose the money but squanders the opportunity to do well. He does nothing and proves himself lazy.

The point of this parable is to do your best with the opportunities given by God. Indeed, that includes using the talents (modern use of the word) in ways that glorify God, but it is not limited to that. We are to use everything God gives us: our homes, money, talents, relationships, intelligence, jobs, schooling, and everything else. God expects his servants to be focused on serving Him with everything they can. Those who do will be rewarded by a God who honors our efforts. Those who do not will be cast out, as is appropriate for a lazy, unworthy, or wicked slave. If they give nothing, nothing will be expected of them.

What do we have that we gained by ourselves without the help of God?

What can we hold back from God?

How would our lives be different if we truly put service for God as the first priority in our lives? What changes would we need to make to do that?

TEN VIRGINS

Matthew 25.1-13

Is there any context for this story? If so, what is it?

Who is speaking and to whom?

Are there other parables around this one or is this one on its own?

Identify where in Jesus's ministry you would place this parable and explain why.
  Beginning • Galilean Ministry • Judean Ministry • Final Weeks

Read the parable in two different translations and note any differences below.

¹ At that time the kingdom of heaven will be like ten virgins who took their lamps and went out to meet the groom. ² Five of them were foolish and five were wise. ³ When the foolish took their lamps, they didn't take oil with them; ⁴ but the wise ones took oil in their flasks with their lamps. ⁵ When the groom was delayed, they all became drowsy and fell asleep.

⁶ "In the middle of the night there was a shout: 'Here's the groom! Come out to meet him.'

⁷ "Then all the virgins got up and trimmed their lamps. ⁸ The foolish ones said to the wise ones, 'Give us some of your oil, because our lamps are going out.'

⁹ "The wise ones answered, 'No, there won't be enough for us and for you. Go instead to those who sell oil, and buy some for yourselves.'

¹⁰ "When they had gone to buy some, the groom arrived, and those who were ready went in with him to the wedding banquet, and the door was shut. ¹¹ Later the rest of the virgins also came and said, 'Master, master, open up for us!'

¹² "He replied, 'Truly I tell you, I don't know you!'

¹³ "Therefore be alert, because you don't know either the day or the hour.

What overall feeling does this story give you?

How many virgins were waiting on the groom?

How many were wise? Why were they wise?

How many were foolish? Why were they foolish?

What happened to the foolish virgins?

Why would the wise virgins not share their oil?

When the foolish virgins returned, what happened?

What is the point of this parable?

This story is confusing unless you have a little background knowledge of wedding feasts from the first century. First, marriages were commonly arranged by families and did not result from "falling in love." These arrangements would result in the signing of a marriage contract between the bride's family and the groom. This contract often set the dowry price, which the groom was then responsible for paying to his wife's family. Once this is signed, they are officially married but are not yet allowed to consummate the marriage until the bride price or dowry is paid. The groom would raise that dowry while preparing a place for the bride. He might build a house or build on his father's house. Once that new home was ready, he would arrange a time with the bride's family to retrieve his wife. He would consummate the marriage, which would then be followed by a wedding feast that could last up to a week, full of celebration and feasting.

The story of the ten virgins is likely about the groom coming to retrieve his wife from the bride's family. They would not know the exact time of his arrival, but they were waiting for him. Since the foolish virgins were not present, they were not allowed in after the gate to the home was closed.

Jesus is our groom and will one day come and retrieve his bride (the church). God will welcome those who are prepared into the celebration.

Was it fair for the groom to exclude these women? Explain your answer.

What are we supposed to learn from this parable? For what are we preparing?

If you could retell this story with modern day traditions or ideas, how would you retell it and teach the same lesson?

Therefore you also must be ready,
for the Son of Man is coming at
an hour you do not expect.
Matthew 24.44

TENANTS

Matthew 21.33-44; Mark 12.1-11; Luke 20.9-18

Is there any context for this story? If so, what is it?

Who is speaking and to whom?

Are there other parables around this one or is this one on its own?

Identify where in Jesus's ministry you would place this parable and explain why.

  Beginning • Galilean Ministry • Judean Ministry • Final Weeks

Read the parable in two different translations and note any differences below.

33 "Listen to another parable: There was a landowner, who planted a vineyard, put a fence around it, dug a winepress in it, and built a watchtower. He leased it to tenant farmers and went away. 34 When the time came to harvest fruit, he sent his servants to the farmers to collect his fruit. 35 The farmers took his servants, beat one, killed another, and stoned a third. 36 Again, he sent other servants, more than the first group, and they did the same to them. 37 Finally, he sent his son to them. 'They will respect my son,' he said.

38 "But when the tenant farmers saw the son, they said to each other, 'This is the heir. Come, let's kill him and take his inheritance.' 39 So they seized him, threw him out of the vineyard, and killed him. 40 Therefore, when the owner of the vineyard comes, what will he do to those farmers?"

41 "He will completely destroy those terrible men," they told him, "and lease his vineyard to other farmers who will give him his fruit at the harvest."

TEXT

QUESTIONS

What overall feeling does this story give you?

What did the landowner plant and build?

Who was supposed to take care of this for the landowner?

How did the landowner check in with the tenants?

What did the tenants do to the servants?

Who did the landowner send last in order to collect his harvest?

What did the tenants do to the son?

What did the tenants think would happen?

What did the landowner do instead?

This is a parable about the kingdom of God. Give your interpretation of this parable.

42 Jesus said to them, "Have you never read in the Scriptures:

The stone that the builders rejected has become the cornerstone.

This is what the Lord has done

and it is wonderful in our eyes?

43 Therefore I tell you, the kingdom of God will be taken away from you and given to a people producing its fruit. 44 Whoever falls on this stone will be broken to pieces; but on whomever it falls, it will shatter him."

Many of the parables left the audience scratching their heads. They were confused about their point. Even the disciples often needed help understanding what Jesus was trying to teach. This was the point of the parables. Jesus sought to help those seeking answers and leave those looking for trouble in the dark.

This parable is an exception. Those who hated Jesus knew precisely what Jesus was teaching and that He was condemning them. They knew that they were the tenant farmers and that Jesus was accusing them of beating and killing the servants. This represented their harsh treatment of the prophets of old, who God sent to deliver messages of judgment and repentance.

Instead of hearing this parable, considering their past, and then seeking to repent, these Jewish leaders were just like their forerunners and sought to kill Jesus. Jesus, the Son, was going to be killed just like the son in the story. Jesus was sent by the land owner to "collect the harvest" of the faithful and instead was beaten and killed by those who were supposed to be watching over the harvest of souls God was growing.

While the Jewish leaders would not have recognized Jesus's claim to be the son of the master in the story, they still recognized their role in his teachings and hated him for it.

Name some of the "servants" the landowner sent in the past. What specifically happened to each one?

Why would these tenant farmers think they would inherit the vineyard if they killed the son?

Jesus quotes Psalm 118.22-23. Read that psalm and describe it below.

TWO SONS

Matthew 21:28-32

Is there any context for this story? If so, what is it?

Who is speaking and to whom?

Are there other parables around this one or is this one on its own?

Identify where in Jesus's ministry you would place this parable and explain why.

   Beginning • Galilean Ministry • Judean Ministry • Final Weeks

Read the parable in two different translations and note any differences below.

28 "What do you think? A man had two sons. He went to the first and said, 'My son, go work in the vineyard today.'

29 "He answered, 'I don't want to,' but later he changed his mind and went. 30 Then the man went to the other and said the same thing. 'I will, sir,' he answered, but he didn't go. 31 Which of the two did his father's will?"

They said, "The first."

Jesus said to them, "Truly I tell you, tax collectors and prostitutes are entering the kingdom of God before you. 32 For John came to you in the way of righteousness, and you didn't believe him. Tax collectors and prostitutes did believe him; but you, when you saw it, didn't even change your minds then and believe him.

What overall feeling does this story give you?

What did the father want his sons to do?

What did the first son say? What did he do?

What did the second son say? What did he do?

Which son obeyed?

What was the point of the parable?

Did the people understand Jesus's parable?

While growing up, my father used to tell a similar adage. He would say that obedience was a matter of will and action. He argued that people must not only do what they were asked to do but also do it with the right attitude.

Interestingly, in Jesus's parable, neither son had the right attitude. One clearly did not want to obey, but he did. The other one says he would, but he clearly does not want to obey, so he does not. Yet, considering the situation Jesus is teaching about, this illustration is perfect.

Jews, the ones who said they would obey but then did not, were not good sons. They refused to follow the God to whom they claimed to be committed. The Gentiles were the ones who initially said no but then came to obey.

When asked, the Jewish audience concluded that the ones who obeyed were the ones who initially said they would not. This means they admitted that the Gentiles were the ones who obeyed. On the tail end of a discussion among the Jews who were too obstinate to realize that Jesus could come from God, this is especially telling. Jesus was revealing that the Jews had rejected themselves and revealed themselves as bad children of God. They refused to obey the commands they had been given generations before, even though they verbally committed themselves to them. They were the disobedient sons.

While we do not see their reaction to this specific parable, we see their reaction after Jesus tells the next parable. Why did they have this reaction?

Which son would you rather be? What third option exists for a son that is even better?

Why are we so tempted to agree but then not follow through with God's commands?

"We must obey God rather than men."

Acts 5.29

UNFRUITFUL FIG TREE

Luke 13:6-9

Is there any context for this story? If so, what is it?

Who is speaking and to whom?

Are there other parables around this one or is this one on its own?

Identify where in Jesus's ministry you would place this parable and explain why.
    Beginning • Galilean Ministry • Judean Ministry • Final Weeks

Read the parable in two different translations and note any differences below.

⁶ And he told this parable: "A man had a fig tree that was planted in his vineyard. He came looking for fruit on it and found none. ⁷ He told the vineyard worker, 'Listen, for three years I have come looking for fruit on this fig tree and haven't found any. Cut it down! Why should it even waste the soil?'

⁸ "But he replied to him, 'Sir, leave it this year also, until I dig around it and fertilize it. ⁹ Perhaps it will produce fruit next year, but if not, you can cut it down.'"

TEXT

What overall feeling does this story give you?

How long was the fig tree barren?

What did the vineyard owner want to do?

What did the owner say the fig tree was doing if it was not producing fruit?

What did his worker convince him to do instead?

What was necessary for the fig tree to produce fruit?

What is the point of this parable?

Anyone who has spent much time in agriculture has experienced the frustration of a barren plant. An apple tree puts on no apples. An orange tree has no fruit. A peach tree gives nothing good to eat.

Sometimes, this barrenness has a reason. Maybe the tree is too young, but this fig tree has had years to produce fruit. Perhaps the tree is under watered, but this tree is in the midst of a vineyard. Maybe the tree has its fruits plucked away by animals, but the owner expects to find fruit. Instead, it seems the problem with this fig tree, if there is any, is that it needs a little more special attention. The worker is willing to do that.

While this can have several applications, it seems the best application is as a story of God's patience. He has been expecting His people to produce fruit year after year, generation after generation. They have not obeyed Him, nor have they produced fruit. Even more specifically, the Jewish leaders have been a consistent problem in God's people's vineyard.

God's ready to chop them down because they are a waste of dirt, but they are given special attention for a short time. This careful attention to feeding and watering them comes from the worker willing to provide them with everything. Jesus Himself becomes their caretaker, but as is revealed in the Gospels, they end up killing the worker who cares for them.

Have you ever been responsible for taking care of a plant or tree? What did you learn about life from doing that?

Why does this worker decide to spend another year on this tree?

What other verses in the Bible speak of God's patience with us?

Take no part in the unfruitful
works of darkness, but instead
expose them.

Ephesians 5.11

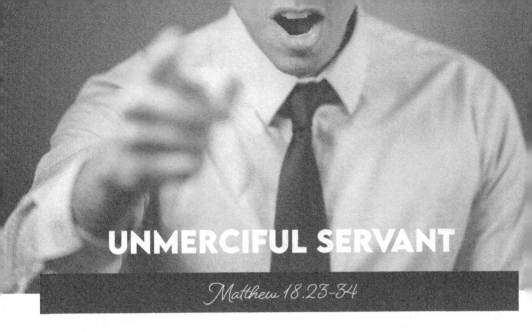

UNMERCIFUL SERVANT

Matthew 18:23-34

Is there any context for this story? If so, what is it?

Who is speaking and to whom?

Are there other parables around this one or is this one on its own?

Identify where in Jesus's ministry you would place this parable and explain why.
   Beginning • Galilean Ministry • Judean Ministry • Final Weeks

Read the parable in two different translations and note any differences below.

23 "For this reason, the kingdom of heaven can be compared to a king who wanted to settle accounts with his servants. 24 When he began to settle accounts, one who owed ten thousand talents was brought before him. 25 Since he did not have the money to pay it back, his master commanded that he, his wife, his children, and everything he had be sold to pay the debt.

26 "At this, the servant fell facedown before him and said, 'Be patient with me, and I will pay you everything.' 27 Then the master of that servant had compassion, released him, and forgave him the loan.

28 "That servant went out and found one of his fellow servants who owed him a hundred denarii. He grabbed him, started choking him, and said, 'Pay what you owe!'

29 "At this, his fellow servant fell down and began begging him, 'Be patient with me, and I will pay you back.' 30 But he wasn't willing. Instead, he went and threw him into prison until he could pay what

What overall feeling does this story give you?

This first servant owed an astronomical amount of debt. If a talent is worth $50,000, how much does he owe?

For what did the servant beg?

How did the master treat his servant?

What surprises you about this interaction?

What did this servant do once he was forgiven?

How much was he owed, if a denarii is worth $350 in today's money?

For what did the second debtor beg?

What response did he receive?

Who tattled?

What did the master do to the first servant?

Was this an appropriate response? Explain your answer.

was owed. [31] When the other servants saw what had taken place, they were deeply distressed and went and reported to their master everything that had happened. [32] Then, after he had summoned him, his master said to him, 'You wicked servant! I forgave you all that debt because you begged me. [33] Shouldn't you also have had mercy on your fellow servant, as I had mercy on you?' [34] And because he was angry, his master handed him over to the jailers to be tortured until he could pay everything that was owed. [35] So also my heavenly Father will do to you unless every one of you forgives his brother or sister from your heart."

The Master was forgiving, and the forgiven was unforgiving. By the end of the parable, both of the indebted are paying their debt in prison. This parable is straightforward: Be forgiving, as all of us have been the recipients of forgiveness. It is easy to see the wickedness of the forgiven servant.

The difficult part of this particular parable is the master's taking back of the servant's forgiveness. When the master becomes displeased with his forgiven servant, he returns the servant's debt to him and throws him in prison. This makes us uncomfortable because, depending on the interpretation, this means God's forgiveness might be conditional. How can we ever be confident in our salvation if God can just return to us all of our guilt and shame?

The truth is that this parable depends on an understanding of patronage from the first century and the context of the master and servant relationship in this story. The master extends grace to this less fortunate man. In this case, the master has been generous enough that the man is beyond any hope of repayment. Then, the master is again generous with forgiving the debt. The proper response to a generous patron is to emulate them in the world and praise them to others. This servant does the opposite and thereby rejects the master's patronage. He dishonors his master through his harshness, and the master is within his rights to punish this servant for his dishonor.

What would be the proper response of this servant to the one who owed him money? Why?

If this wicked servant had money owed to him, should he not have tried to get that money so he could pay back his master? Is that what is happening in this parable?

If you were hearing this parable for the first time, what moments in the story are shocking? Explain.

WATCHFUL SERVANTS

Luke 12.35-40

Is there any context for this story? If so, what is it?

Who is speaking and to whom?

Are there other parables around this one or is this one on its own?

Identify where in Jesus's ministry you would place this parable and explain why.
Beginning • Galilean Ministry • Judean Ministry • Final Weeks

Read the parable in two different translations and note any differences below.

TEXT

35 "Be ready for service and have your lamps lit. 36 You are to be like people waiting for their master to return from the wedding banquet so that when he comes and knocks, they can open the door for him at once. 37 Blessed will be those servants the master finds alert when he comes. Truly I tell you, he will get ready, have them recline at the table, then come and serve them. 38 If he comes in the middle of the night, or even near dawn, and finds them alert, blessed are those servants. 39 But know this: If the homeowner had known at what hour the thief was coming, he would not have let his house be broken into. 40 You also be ready, because the Son of Man is coming at an hour you do not expect."

QUESTIONS

What overall feeling does this story give you?

What does it mean to "have your lamps lit?" What other parable does this remind you of?

Where has the master been?

What should the servants be doing while the master is away?

What does the master expect when he comes home in the middle of the night?

What does the master do for his servants when he finds them waiting?

When will the Son of Man come?

There is an interesting contrast between this parable and the one in Luke 17.7-10. As a modern person with a contemporary understanding of God, we accept the presentation of the Master in this parable much more quickly. Yet, the Jew from the first century would be much more comfortable with the presentation of the master in Luke 17. In our modern culture, we appreciate fairness, kindness, and the support of the less fortunate. The concept of a master who would be demanding after "work hours" sounds harsh and outrageous to us. The master who would come in and serve others who had pleased him makes sense to us.

This parable would have been much more scandalous to the original audience. Masters were not to serve their servants; it would have been beneath them. Servants should not expect such preferential treatment.

Yet, Jesus had a habit of turning expectations upside down. He liked to make the despised heroes, and he liked to present the counter-cultural nature of the Kingdom and the King. This Master, who represents our King, is a kind-hearted, fair-minded, and compassion-showing Master. He is Yahweh.

This master's behavior was so shocking that the apostles responded, "Why would you tell us this? Is this a teaching for only us? Do you want everyone to hear this message?" (author's paraphrase). Jesus did want everyone to know that God was a God who served others, so much so that He served others so publicly that He hung on a cross for them.

How does this parable compare to the parable in Luke 17.7-10?

Does this kind of Master comfort you? Have you considered the flip side of what the Master will do if his servants had not been faithful?

Find verses throughout the Bible that describe God the way Jesus describes the Master in this parable.

Be sober-minded; be watchful.

1 Peter 5.8

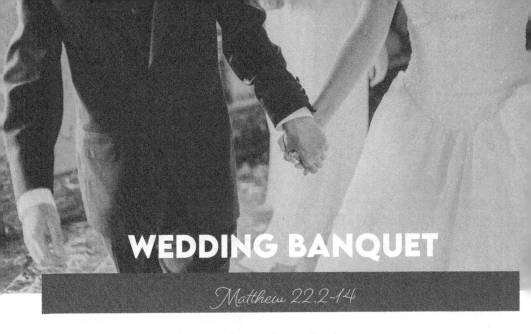

WEDDING BANQUET

Matthew 22.2-14

Is there any context for this story? If so, what is it?

Who is speaking and to whom?

Are there other parables around this one or is this one on its own?

Identify where in Jesus's ministry you would place this parable and explain why.
   Beginning • Galilean Ministry • Judean Ministry • Final Weeks

Read the parable in two different translations and note any differences below.

2 "The kingdom of heaven is like a king who gave a wedding banquet for his son. 3 He sent his servants to summon those invited to the banquet, but they didn't want to come. 4 Again, he sent out other servants and said, 'Tell those who are invited: See, I've prepared my dinner; my oxen and fattened cattle have been slaughtered, and everything is ready. Come to the wedding banquet.'

5 "But they paid no attention and went away, one to his own farm, another to his business, 6 while the rest seized his servants, mistreated them, and killed them. 7 The king was enraged, and he sent out his troops, killed those murderers, and burned down their city.

8 "Then he told his servants, 'The banquet is ready, but those who were invited were not worthy. 9 Go then to where the roads exit the city and invite everyone you find to the banquet.' 10 So those servants went out on the roads and gathered everyone they found, both evil and good.

QUESTIONS

What overall feeling does this story give you?

What kind of part is the master throwing?

Who did he invite?

What was their response?

What did they do to the servants who announced that the banquet was ready?

How did the king respond to those who were invited?

Since those who were invited did not come, where did they find guests for the wedding?

Since the wedding had strangers attending, how does it describe those strangers?

When the king came, was he pleased? Why?

What did the king do to the improperly dressed man?

What does verse 14 mean?

The wedding banquet was filled with guests. [11] When the king came in to see the guests, he saw a man there who was not dressed for a wedding. [12] So he said to him, 'Friend, how did you get in here without wedding clothes?' The man was speechless.

[13] "Then the king told the attendants, 'Tie him up hand and foot, and throw him into the outer darkness, where there will be weeping and gnashing of teeth.'

[14] "For many are invited, but few are chosen."

This parable displays a lot of unexpected violence. The setting is a wedding feast, so you expect things to be happy and celebratory. Instead, the invited were violent towards the servants who invited them. The king is violent towards those who mistreat his servants. The king was then violent towards the improperly dressed man. The entire parable is unsettling.

Yet, what stands out most in this parable is the treatment of the improperly dressed man. The wedding is filled with those who were not initially invited. These are strangers. These people show up for the feast more than they do to support a marriage. There should be a low expectation. Yet, in this case, the king still expects those who show up to be appropriately dressed and ready for the banquet.

When the king throws out the man for his impropriety, he throws him to a place of outer darkness. This refers to hell, which becomes our clue that this parable is not really about a wedding feast but something much more important. No one is imprisoned for wearing the wrong clothes to a party. But what about someone who comes to God but does not live and act like he belongs to God? It reminds us of Peter's strong words in 2 Peter 2.20-22. When we come to God, we must make a true effort to belong to God.

Do you think this king is harsh? Explain your answer.

Why would those invited to the feast have such a strong reaction? Who does this represent in real life? Explain your answer.

This feast had evil and good people at it. It had an improperly dressed man. This means there are people at the wedding feast that could not be in heaven. If this is not talking about heaven, what is it talking about?

WEEDS

Matthew 13:24-30

Is there any context for this story? If so, what is it?

Who is speaking and to whom?

Are there other parables around this one or is this one on its own?

Identify where in Jesus's ministry you would place this parable and explain why.
 Beginning • Galilean Ministry • Judean Ministry • Final Weeks

Read the parable in two different translations and note any differences below.

24 He presented another parable to them: "The kingdom of heaven may be compared to a man who sowed good seed in his field. 25 But while people were sleeping, his enemy came, sowed weeds among the wheat, and left. 26 When the plants sprouted and produced grain, then the weeds also appeared. 27 The landowner's servants came to him and said, 'Master, didn't you sow good seed in your field? Then where did the weeds come from?'

28 "'An enemy did this,' he told them.

"'So, do you want us to go and pull them up?' the servants asked him.

29 "'No,' he said. 'When you pull up the weeds, you might also uproot the wheat with them. 30 Let both grow together until the harvest. At harvest time I'll tell the reapers: Gather the weeds first and tie them in bundles to burn them, but collect the wheat in my barn.'"

TEXT

QUESTIONS

What overall feeling does this story give you?

What did the man sow?

What did he expect to reap?

What did his enemy sow?

Why did he do this?

When did the servants realize what had happened?

Why did the farmer not want to pull the weeds?

When would the bad and the good plants be separated?

Good and bad seeds are being sown in the kingdom, and good and bad plants are being grown in the kingdom. The field is said to be the world, but the world is reflected in the Kingdom. The parable is clear that the church is filled with people who are good and evil. In the church, some people are pretending to be good. They are there because of heritage because their spouse expects them to be, or because it is what they have always known. They look good from the outside, pretending to be holy and righteous, but inside, they are rotten with sin. They are addicted to evil. They have never submitted to God's reign or humbled themselves for God's help. They are not genuinely pursuing God's will but only when it aligns with their desires. The truth is that this can be a description of any of us. All of us can be selfish, harsh, prideful, and sinful. All of us can be bad seeds.

Yet, in the church, God allows us to remain until the harvest or until the judgment. This means that God is aware of what is in our hearts and that God is patient, not wishing for any to perish (2 Pet 3.9). He is giving all people a chance to be good.

Some will change because of their interactions with the perfect seed. Many will not. Only God knows which will be harvested for the barn and which will be harvested for the fire. Until this day, whenever it happens, we are left with the choice. Are we going to be a good seed? Hopefully, we can be self-aware enough to know which side of the harvest we belong on (cf. Mat 7.2312-23).

The enemy sows bad seed among the crops. Who is the enemy?

What danger exists in the church by God leaving the weeds with the wheat?

What benefits exists in the church by God leaving the weeds with the wheat?

Are you weeds or wheat? Explain.

*Do not be unequally yoked
with unbelievers. For what
partnership has righteousness with
lawlessness? Or what fellowship
has light with darkness?*

2 Corinthians 6.14

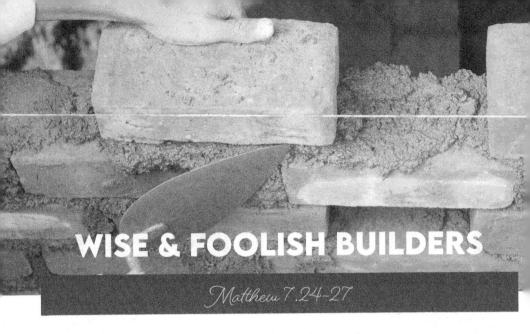

WISE & FOOLISH BUILDERS

Matthew 7.24-27

Is there any context for this story? If so, what is it?

Who is speaking and to whom?

Are there other parables around this one or is this one on its own?

Identify where in Jesus's ministry you would place this parable and explain why.
Beginning • Galilean Ministry • Judean Ministry • Final Weeks

Read the parable in two different translations and note any differences below.

TEXT

24 "Therefore, everyone who hears these words of mine and acts on them will be like a wise man who built his house on the rock. 25 The rain fell, the rivers rose, and the winds blew and pounded that house. Yet it didn't collapse, because its foundation was on the rock. 26 But everyone who hears these words of mine and doesn't act on them will be like a foolish man who built his house on the sand. 27 The rain fell, the rivers rose, the winds blew and pounded that house, and it collapsed. It collapsed with a great crash."

QUESTIONS

What overall feeling does this story give you?

What are these two men both doing?

The wise man built where?

What happened to his house?

The foolish man built where?

What happened to his house?

Jesus tells this parable at the end of his Sermon on the Mount (cf. Matt 5-7). Why would this parable be appropriate for that setting?

A well-built foundation is essential for two reasons. First, they become the steady and sturdy floor on which the entire house is built. A firm foundation makes a house able to not shift. Everything built in place stays in place because the foundation is sure.

Second, the foundation often included a cornerstone. This was the first stone that was put in place. Every other stone of the foundation was measured and leveled against this stone. Every wall is put up based on the measurements of this stone. The roof was built straight because it was measured off this stone. This stone became the most important part of the house while it was being built.

Interestingly, the difference between a solid or soft foundation in Jesus's story was not whether a person heard the word of God. Both the wise and the foolish man listened to the word of God. The difference was whether they obeyed it. The wise man heard and did the teachings. The foolish man heard but ignored them. The difference was not the presence of God's Word but the presence of obedience.

This parable fights back in a religious world that wants to argue that faith is only what you believe. Belief is the beginning point, but action is the difference between wisdom and foolhardiness. We must hear, apply, and obey God's Word, building our lives based on His truth.

Jesus is clear that wisdom is not merely understanding, but doing. Name some of the fools that Jesus dealt with in His ministry.

What happened to both houses that put them at risk? What does this mean for us today?

Why does knowing and obeying God's word give us strength, sturdiness, and steadiness in life? Do you struggle with this?

Unless the Lord builds the house,
those who build it labor in vain.

Psalm 127.1

WISE AND FOOLISH SERVANTS

Luke 12:42-48

Is there any context for this story? If so, what is it?

Who is speaking and to whom?

Are there other parables around this one or is this one on its own?

Identify where in Jesus's ministry you would place this parable and explain why.
  Beginning • Galilean Ministry • Judean Ministry • Final Weeks

Read the parable in two different translations and note any differences below.

⁴² The Lord said, "Who then is the faithful and sensible manager his master will put in charge of his household servants to give them their allotted food at the proper time? ⁴³ Blessed is that servant whom the master finds doing his job when he comes. ⁴⁴ Truly I tell you, he will put him in charge of all his possessions. ⁴⁵ But if that servant says in his heart, 'My master is delaying his coming,' and starts to beat the male and female servants, and to eat and drink and get drunk, ⁴⁶ that servant's master will come on a day he does not expect him and at an hour he does not know. He will cut him to pieces and assign him a place with the unfaithful. ⁴⁷ And that servant who knew his master's will and didn't prepare himself or do it will be severely beaten. ⁴⁸ But the one who did not know and did what deserved punishment will receive a light beating. From everyone who has been given much, much will be required; and from the one who has been entrusted with much, even more will be expected.

TEXT

QUESTIONS

What overall feeling does this story give you?

Who will the master put in charge?

Who is blessed?

How is the foolish servant described in this passage?

Why does he behave this way?

What will happen to the foolish servant?

What can those who know better but choose worse expect?

What is required from those who have been given much?

We tend to act based on our environment. We are taught to do this. We are typically quieter in a library than at a football game. We act crazy at a party but are studious in a classroom. We will behave one way with our parents present and behave differently when we are surrounded by friends. The good part of this is that it shows discretion and propriety.

The bad part is that it can lead to disingenuous decision-making and a lack of integrity. We can learn to be two-faced and inconsistent in our lives. When we act righteous in front of our parents but unrighteous when they are not around, we show that we are not truly virtuous. We are being insincere when we talk one way in the classroom and another in the locker room.

James addresses this in 3.10-12 when teaching about our speech. Jesus also addresses it in the Sermon on the Mount (Matt 7.17-23). We cannot serve two masters at once (6.24) or be two different things at the same time.

These foolish slaves failed to have integrity. They would pretend to be good servants when the master was present and act differently when they knew the master would be away.

The reality for us is that our Master is never away. He never sleeps nor slumbers (Psalm 121.4). He sees all, but luckily, He also forgives all and loves us. Be a person of integrity, and you need not worry about when He sees you.

What makes the good servants good? What can they expect? How does this relate to us today?

What makes the bad servants bad? What can they expect? How does this relate to us today?

If God sees everything we do, how should this change our behavior? How should this change our decision-making? Should this give us confidence or worry?

Whoever trusts in his own mind is a fool, but he who walks in wisdom will be delivered.

Proverbs 28.26

WORKERS IN THE VINEYARD

Matthew 20.1-16

Is there any context for this story? If so, what is it?

Who is speaking and to whom?

Are there other parables around this one or is this one on its own?

Identify where in Jesus's ministry you would place this parable and explain why.

   Beginning • Galilean Ministry • Judean Ministry • Final Weeks

Read the parable in two different translations and note any differences below.

TEXT

¹ "For the kingdom of heaven is like a landowner who went out early in the morning to hire workers for his vineyard. ² After agreeing with the workers on one denarius, he sent them into his vineyard for the day. ³ When he went out about nine in the morning, he saw others standing in the marketplace doing nothing. ⁴ He said to them, 'You also go into my vineyard, and I'll give you whatever is right.' So off they went. ⁵ About noon and about three, he went out again and did the same thing. ⁶ Then about five he went and found others standing around and said to them, 'Why have you been standing here all day doing nothing?'

⁷ "'Because no one hired us,' they said to him.

"'You also go into my vineyard,' he told them. ⁸ When evening came, the owner of the vineyard told his foreman, 'Call the workers and give them their pay, starting with the last and ending with the first.'

⁹ "When those who were hired about five came,

QUESTIONS

What overall feeling does this story give you?

When did the first workers start working? How long did they work and for how much?

When did the second group of workers start working? How long did they work and for how much?

When did the third group of workers start working? How long did they work and for how much?

When did the fourth group of workers start working? How long did they work and for how much?

Why had the last group of workers not been working?

When the end of the day came, they were all paid. How much was each group paid?

Was this fair? Explain your answer.

What complaint did the master hear? What was his response?

How does the master describe himself? Do you agree?

Who was mistreated in this story?

What does verse 16 mean?

they each received one denarius. 10 So when the first ones came, they assumed they would get more, but they also received a denarius each. 11 When they received it, they began to complain to the landowner: 12 'These last men put in one hour, and you made them equal to us who bore the burden of the day's work and the burning heat.'

13 "He replied to one of them, 'Friend, I'm doing you no wrong. Didn't you agree with me on a denarius? 14 Take what's yours and go. I want to give this last man the same as I gave you. 15 Don't I have the right to do what I want with what is mine? Are you jealous because I'm generous?'

16 "So the last will be first, and the first last."

As a people, we have a sense of ought, meaning we innately think we know how things should be. We define what we believe ought to happen as correct and determine what we think ought not to be wrong.

In this parable, Jesus plays with our sense of ought. Most of us would agree with the workers who worked all day. The "right" thing is for them to be paid more than those who only worked for one hour. We feel sorry for those who worked all day. But they were paid what they agreed to be paid.

The problem with our sense of "ought" is that it sometimes changes based on the situation. The workers hired at the beginning of the day probably considered themselves lucky. They found work. They were to be paid a fair wage (a denarius was the fair pay for a day's labor). They were going to be able to work and feed their families. They were luckier than those left behind without work for the day.

When they went to be paid, those same workers felt cheated because they were not paid more than those who worked only an hour. Their luck had not changed at all. Their situation changed, which means their perspective changed, and therefore, their sense of ought changed.

In this parable, Jesus warns us to be careful not to measure right and wrong based on our feelings or situations but on what is truly right and wrong.

How would you feel if you were "underpaid" compared to someone else at work, especially if they were not working as hard as you?

Why do we struggle so much with our sense of fairness? Has your sense that something was "wrong" ever changed your behavior, thoughts, or attitude?

Do you agree that the master is generous? Explain your answer.

HOW TO USE THIS BOOK IN A
CLASSROOM SETTING

This book is designed for personal use, but this does not mean that it cannot be a welcome addition to a Bible Class program at a local congregation. It can be used for adults or teens. We designed it to create conversation.

Because we designed this book for personal use, we did not fill it with long pages of discussion questions. Each parable has easy-to-answer questions that allow for observation of the text and a few thought questions.

Our recommendation for classroom use is to pay special attention to the first page of context-related questions. This is the part that is easy for students to skip over when approaching a topic like parables, but it is the part that makes it possible to understand Jesus's intent in telling these stories. People often neglect exploring the context.

Second, we recommend that you come up with your own thought questions in addition to the ones found in each lesson. You can find these in other workbooks, but we encourage teachers to dwell on the passages themselves in such a way that they come up with their own questions.

Third, because there are forty lessons, this does not fit within most congregation's class schedules. Pick and choose which lessons and parables you want to cover, but let the class know ahead of time so they can read, prepare, and be ready for discussion. Prepared students make better classes.

Fourth, pray, pray, pray. This is not specific to this lesson book but to all studies of God's Word. We often neglect the role of prayer and God's softening of hearts to His Word. Prayer is always a welcome addition before class begins, when class ends, and in preparation for class.

We hope these lessons bless you, your students, and your congregation. God's Word always has a way of breaking through to the hard places of our hearts when we allow it. We pray it will do this in your and your students' study of the parables.

Made in the USA
Monee, IL
14 January 2025

76872048R00098